Daily Telegraph

ATHLETICS

KEN MAYS

T

Consultant Editor: Norman Barrett

Editor: Gill Freeman

Design: Nigel Standerline

Designed and produced by
Autumn Publishing Ltd.,
10 Eastgate Square, Chichester,
West Sussex.

Published by Telegraph Publications,
135, Fleet Street,
London EC4P 4BL

Acknowledgements

It has been my good fortune to have among my
friends top-class coach Tom McNab and three of
the most knowledgeable people in athletics, Mel
Watman, Peter Matthews, and Stan Greenberg
— a walking hat-trick when it comes to facts and
figures on this wonderful sport. It is to them I owe
much credit in being able to compile this book,
for I have referred constantly to their superb
publications: McNab's *The Complete Book of
Athletics* (Ward Lock), Greenberg's *Guinness
Book of Olympic Facts and Feats*, Matthews'
Guinness Book of Athletics Facts and Feats, and
Watman's *Encyclopaedia of Track and Field
Athletics* (Hale).

My thanks also to Gill Freeman for her
patience, and to everyone who has made
athletics so enjoyable.

© 1984 Daily Telegraph
and Autumn Publishing Ltd.

Typesetting by Project Reprographics, Chichester.
Printed by CGP Delo, Yugoslavia.

ISBN 0 86367 019 9

CONTENTS

INTRODUCTION

With the advent of the first World Championships in 1983 and the ability now of athletes legally to build up a financial nest-egg for their retirement, the sport of athletics is really booming. Add to this the proliferation of 'people's marathons' and 'fun runs' and you have a sport that, while always capable of hitting the headlines when the likes of Jesse Owens, Zatopek, Herb Elliott, Coe, Ovett, Cram, or Mary Decker are around, has reached new heights in popularity and participation worldwide. Other current stars who have ensured their place among the sport's 'immortals' include Carl Lewis, Daley Thomson, Greta Waitz, and Jarmila Kratochvilova. And the sporting heroes and heroines from Russia and East Germany are almost too numerous to mention. The little countries, too, never cease to surprise with the talent they produce. It is interesting to note that Finland — always a great athletics nation — and New Zealand have each provided three Olympic 1,500 metres champions, and Ireland and Luxembourg one each. The Finns Paavo Nurmi and Lasse Viren are among the top few middle distance runners of all time. And African countries have been in the forefront of world athletics since the 1960s, when Ethiopia's Abebe Bikila and Kenya's Kip Keino emerged as brilliant champions. Other 'greats' such as Miruts Yifter and Henry Rono have followed in their footsteps. Now that China — already with a world record high jumper in Jianhua Zhu — has rejoined the international fold, who knows what lies in store? Interest has never been higher.

Squeezing the facts and figures of athletics into a pocket book necessitates much distillation. By tracing the sport's development through its personalities and their performances, we have sought to provide a guide to modern athletics and a valuable, handy work of reference.

The view of the World Championships is a personal one, and I admit, even after covering athletics round the world for the *Daily Telegraph* for many years, that I still feel the emotions of the occasion. The delight of seeing Steve Cram finally make it to the top — although I had fancied Steve Ovett to win — and the disappointment when Seb Coe withdrew through illness, are contrasting memories that will always be with me.

The records of the Olympics, European Championships, Commonwealth Games, and other major events have been set out to make it easy to compare form and enable interesting patterns to emerge — to see just which athletes and countries have dominated particular events. Many of the great names appear in the biographical section, although, for reasons of space, many others have had to be omitted.

In the section on the evolution of world records, only times officially reported and recognized by the International Amateur Athletic Federation have been included. Indeed, we are of the opinion that if they were not reported, then all

4

cannot have been right at the time. It is worthwhile to compare the leaps and bounds in improvement in the early days of the records, and again when the use of synthetic tracks came into being, with the gradual slow-down as the peak of physical performances are reached.

We have also tried to explain the rules in simple fashion, and how an amateur can get so much money in a legal way today. In other words, we have endeavoured to provide the answers to the questions that arise for the active club athlete, the enthusiastic spectator, and the armchair fan, and to settle the friendly arguments that occur whenever the exciting and varied sport of athletics is discussed.

Carl Lewis (USA) winning the sprint relay at the World Championships in Helsinki.

PROGRESSIVE WORLD RECORDS

MEN

100 metres

sec

10.6	D Lippincott	US	Stockholm	6 Jul	1912
10.6	J Scholz	US	Stockholm	6 Sep	1912
10.4	C Paddock	US	Redlands	23 Apr	1921
10.4	E Tolan	US	Stockholm	8 Aug	1929
10.4	E Tolan	US	Copenhagen	15 Aug	1929
10.3	P Williams	Canada	Toronto	9 Aug	1930
10.3	E Tolan	US	Los Angeles	1 Aug	1932
10.3	R Metcalfe	US	Budapest	12 Aug	1933
10.3	E Peacock	US	Oslo	6 Aug	1934
10.3	C Berger	Netherlands	Amsterdam	26 Aug	1934
10.3	R Metcalfe	US	Osaka	15 Sep	1934
10.3	R Metcalfe	US	Dairen	23 Sep	1934
10.3	T Yoshioka	Japan	Tokyo	15 Jun	1935
10.2	J Owens	US	Chicago	20 Jun	1936
10.2	H Davis	US	Compton	6 Jun	1941
10.2	L LaBeach	Panama	Fresno	15 May	1948
10.2	N Ewell	US	Evanston	9 Jul	1948
10.2	E McDonald Bailey	GB	Belgrade	25 Aug	1951
10.2	H Futterer	Germany	Yokohama	31 Oct	1954
10.2	B Morrow	US	Houston	19 May	1956
10.2	I Murchison	US	Compton	1 Jun	1956
10.2	B Morrow	US	Bakersfield	22 Jun	1956
10.2	I Murchison	US	Los Angeles	29 Jun	1956
10.2	B Morrow	US	Los Angeles	29 Jun	1956
10.1	W Williams	US	Berlin	3 Aug	1956
10.1	I Murchison	US	Berlin	4 Aug	1956
10.1	L King	US	Ontario	20 Oct	1956
10.1	L King	US	Santa Ana	27 Oct	1956
10.1	R Norton	US	San José	18 Apr	1959
10.0	A Hary	Germany	Zürich	21 Jun	1960
10.0	H Jerome	Canada	Saskatoon	15 Jul	1960
10.0	H Esteves	Venezuela	Caracas	15 Aug	1964
10.0	B Hayes	US	Tokyo	15 Oct	1964
10.0	J Hines	US	Modesto	27 May	1967
10.0	P Nash	S Africa	Krugersdorp	2 Apr	1968
10.0	O Ford	US	Albuquerque	31 May	1968
10.0	C Greene	US	Sacramento	10 Jun	1968
10.0	R Bambuck	France	Sacramento	20 Jun	1968
9.9	J Hines	US	Sacramento	10 Jun	1968
9.9	R Ray Smith	US	Sacramento	20 Jun	1968
9.9	C Greene	US	Sacramento	20 Jun	1968
9.9	J Hines	US	Mexico	14 Oct	1968

Evolution of world records as ratified by the International Amateur Athletic Federation since its inception in 1913.

9.9	E Hart	US	Eugene	1 Jul	1972
9.9	R Robinson	US	Eugene	1 Jul	1972
9.9	S Williams	US	Westwood	21 Jun	1974
9.9	S Leonard	Cuba	Ostrava	5 Jun	1975
9.9	S Williams	US	Siena	16 Jul	1975
9.9	S Williams	US	Berlin	22 Aug	1975
9.9	S Williams	US	Gainesville	27 Mar	1976
9.9	H Glance	US	Columbia	3 Apr	1976
9.9	H Glance	US	Baton Rouge	1 May	1976
9.9	D Quarrie	Jamaica	Modesto	22 May	1976
Automatic Timing since 1 May 1977					
9.93	C Smith	US	Colorado Springs	3 Jul	1983

200 metres

sec

20.6	A Stanfield	US	Philadelphia	26 May	1951
20.6	A Stanfield	US	Los Angeles	28 Jun	1952
20.6	T Baker	US	Bakersfield	23 Jun	1956
20.6	B Morrow	US	Melbourne	27 Nov	1956
20.6	M Germar	West Germany	Wuppertal	1 Oct	1958
20.6	R Norton	US	Berkeley	19 Mar	1960
20.6	R Norton	US	Philadelphia	30 Apr	1960
20.5	P Radford	GB	Wolverhampton	28 May	1960
20.5	S Johnson	US	Palo Alto	2 Jul	1960
20.5	R Norton	US	Palo Alto	2 Jul	1960
20.5	L Berruti	Italy	Rome	3 Sep	1960
20.5	L Berruti	Italy	Rome	3 Sep	1960
20.5	P Drayton	US	Walnut	23 Jun	1962
20.3	H Carr	US	Tempe	23 Mar	1963
20.2	H Carr	US	Tempe	4 Apr	1964
20.0	T Smith	US	Sacramento	11 Jun	1966
19.8	T Smith	US	Mexico	16 Oct	1968
19.8	D Quarrie	Jamaica	Cali	3 Aug	1971
19.8	D Quarrie	Jamaica	Eugene	7 Jun	1975
Automatic Timing since 1 May 1977					
19.83	T Smith	US	Mexico	16 Oct	1968
19.72	P Mennea	Italy	Mexico	12 Sep	1979

400 metres

sec

47.8*	M Long	US	New York	29 Sep	1900
47.4*	T Meredith	US	Cambridge	27 May	1916
47.0	E Spencer	US	Palo Alto	12 May	1928
46.4*	B Eastman	US	Palo Alto	26 Mar	1932

46.2	B Carr	US	Los Angeles	5 Aug 1932
46.1	A Williams	US	Chicago	19 Jun 1936
46.0	R Harbig	Germany	Frankfurt	12 Aug 1939
46.0	G Klemmer	US	Philadelphia	29 Jun 1941
46.3*	H McKenley	Jamaica	Berkeley	28 Jun 1947
46.0*	H McKenley	Jamaica	Berkeley	5 Jun 1948
45.9	H McKenley	Jamaica	Milwaukee	2 Jul 1948
45.8	G Rhoden	Jamaica	Eskilstuna	22 Aug 1950
45.4	L Jones	US	Mexico	18 Mar 1955
45.2	L Jones	US	Los Angeles	30 Jun 1956
44.9	O Davis	US	Rome	6 Sep 1960
44.9	C Kaufmann	West Germany	Rome	6 Sep 1960
44.9*	A Plummer	US	Tempe	25 May 1963
44.9	M Larrabee	US	Los Angeles	12 Sep 1964
44.5	T Smith	US	San José	20 May 1967
44.1	L James	US	Echo Summit	14 Sep 1968
43.8	L Evans	US	Mexico	18 Oct 1968

Automatic Timing since 1 May 1977

43.86	L Evans	US	Mexico	18 Oct 1968

* timed over 440 yards (402.34 metres)

800 metres

min sec

1 51.9	T Meredith	US	Stockholm	8 Jul 1912
1 52.2*	T Meredith	US	Philadelphia	13 May 1916
1 51.6*	O Peltzer	Germany	London	3 Jul 1926
1 50.6	S Martin	France	Colombes	14 Jul 1928
1 49.8	T Hampson	GB	Los Angeles	2 Aug 1932
1 49.8	B Eastman	US	Princeton	16 Jun 1934
1 49.7	G Cunningham	US	Stockholm	20 Aug 1936
1 49.6	E Robinson	US	New York	11 Jul 1937
1 48.4	S Wooderson	GB	Motspur Park	20 Aug 1938
1 46.6	R Harbig	Germany	Milan	15 Jul 1939
1 45.7	R Moens	Belgium	Oslo	3 Aug 1955
1 44.3	P Snell	NZ	Christchurch	3 Feb 1962
1 44.9	J Ryun	US	Terre Haute	10 Jun 1966
1 44.3	R Doubell	Australia	Mexico	15 Oct 1968
1 44.3	D Wottle	US	Eugene	1 Jul 1972
1 44.6	R Wohlhuter	US	Los Angeles	27 May 1973
1 43.7	M Fiasconaro	Italy	Milan	27 Jun 1973
1 44.1	R Wohlhuter	US	Eugene	8 Jun 1974
1 43.50	A Juantorena	Cuba	Montreal	25 Jul 1976
1 43.44	A Juantorena	Cuba	Sofia	21 Aug 1977
1 42.33	S Coe	GB	Oslo	5 Jul 1979
1 41.73	S Coe	GB	Florence	10 Jun 1981

* timed over 880 yards (804.67 metres)

1,500 metres

min sec

min sec	Name	Country	Place	Date
3 55.8	A Kiviat	US	Cambridge, US	8 Jun 1912
3 54.7	J Zander	Sweden	Stockholm	5 Aug 1917
3 52.6	P Nurmi	Finland	Helsinki	19 Jun 1924
3 51.0	O Peltzer	Germany	Berlin	11 Sep 1926
3 49.2	J Ladoumègue	France	Paris	5 Oct 1930
3 49.2	L Beccali	Italy	Turin	9 Sep 1933
3 49.0	L Beccali	Italy	Milan	17 Sep 1933
3 48.8	B Bonthron	US	Milwaukee	30 Jun 1934
3 47.8	J Lovelock	NZ	Berlin	6 Aug 1936
3 47.6	G Hagg	Sweden	Stockholm	10 Aug 1941
3 45.8	G Hagg	Sweden	Stockholm	17 Jul 1942
3 45.0	A Andersson	Sweden	Gothenburg	17 Aug 1943
3 43.0	G Hagg	Sweden	Gothenburg	7 Jul 1944
3 43.0	L Strand	Sweden	Malmo	15 Jul 1947
3 43.0	W Lueg	Germany	Berlin	29 Jun 1952
3 42.8	W Santee	US	Compton	4 Jun 1954
3 41.8	J Landy	Australia	Turku	21 Jun 1954
3 40.8	S Iharos	Hungary	Helsinki	28 Jul 1955
3 40.8	L Tabori	Hungary	Oslo	6 Sep 1955
3 40.8	G Nielsen	Denmark	Oslo	6 Sep 1955
3 40.6	I Rozsavolgyi	Hungary	Tata	3 Aug 1956
3 40.2	O Salsola	Finland	Turku	11 Jul 1957
3 40.2	O Salonen	Finland	Turku	11 Jul 1957
3 38.1	S Jungwirth	Czech	Stara Boleslav	12 Jul 1957
3 36.0	H Elliott	Australia	Gothenburg	28 Aug 1958
3 35.6	H Elliott	Australia	Rome	6 Sep 1960
3 33.1	J Ryun	US	Los Angeles	8 Jul 1967
3 32.16	F Bayi	Tanzania	Christchurch	2 Feb 1974
3 32.03	S Coe	GB	Zürich	15 Aug 1979
3 32.09	S Ovett	GB	Oslo	15 Jul 1980
3 31.36	S Ovett	GB	Koblenz	27 Aug 1980
3 31.24	S Maree	US	Cologne	28 Aug 1983
3 30.77	S Ovett	GB	Rieti	4 Sep 1983

Mile

min sec

min sec	Name	Country	Place	Date
4 14.4	JP Jones	US	Cambridge, US	31 May 1913
4 12.6	N Taber	US	Cambridge, US	16 Jul 1915
4 10.4	P Nurmi	Finland	Stockholm	23 Aug 1923
4 09.2	J Ladoumègue	France	Paris	4 Oct 1931
4 07.6	J Lovelock	NZ	Princeton	15 Jul 1933
4 06.8	G Cunningham	US	Princeton	16 Jun 1934
4 06.4	S Wooderson	GB	Motspur Park	28 Aug 1937
4 06.2	G Hagg	Sweden	Gothenburg	1 Jul 1942
4 06.2	A Andersson	Sweden	Stockholm	10 Jul 1942
4 04.6	G Hagg	Sweden	Stockholm	4 Sep 1942
4 02.6	A Andersson	Sweden	Gothenburg	1 Jul 1943
4 01.6	A Andersson	Sweden	Malmo	18 Jul 1944

4 01.4	G Hagg	Sweden	Malmo	17 Jul	1945
3 59.4	R Bannister	GB	Oxford	6 May	1954
3 58.0	J Landy	Australia	Turku	21 Jun	1954
3 57.2	D Ibbotson	GB	London	19 Jul	1957
3 54.5	H Elliott	Australia	Dublin	6 Aug	1958
3 54.4	P Snell	NZ	Wanganui	27 Jan	1962
3 54.1	P Snell	NZ	Auckland	17 Nov	1964
3 53.6	M Jazy	France	Rennes	9 Jun	1965
3 51.3	J Ryun	US	Berkeley	17 Jul	1966
3 51.1	J Ryun	US	Bakersfield	23 Jun	1967
3 51.0	F Bayi	Tanzania	Kingston	17 May	1975
3 49.4	J Walker	NZ	Gothenburg	12 Aug	1975
3 48.95	S Coe	GB	Oslo	17 Jul	1979
3 48.8	S Ovett	GB	Oslo	1 Jul	1980
3 48.53	S Coe	GB	Zürich	19 Aug	1981
3 48.40	S Ovett	GB	Koblenz	26 Aug	1981
3 47.33	S Coe	GB	Brussels	28 Aug	1981

5,000 metres

min sec

14 36.6	H Kolehmainen	Finland	Stockholm	10 Jul	1912
14 35.4	P Nurmi	Finland	Stockholm	12 Sep	1922
14 28.2	P Nurmi	Finland	Helsinki	19 Jun	1924
14 17.0	L Lehtinen	Finland	Helsinki	19 Jun	1932
14 08.8	T Maki	Finland	Helsinki	16 Jun	1939
13 58.2	G Hagg	Sweden	Gothenburg	20 Sep	1942
13 57.2	E Zátopek	Czech	Colombes	30 May	1954
13 56.6	V Kuts	USSR	Berne	29 Aug	1954
13 51.6	C Chataway	GB	London	13 Oct	1954
13 51.2	V Kuts	USSR	Prague	23 Oct	1954
13 50.8	S Iharos	Hungary	Budapest	10 Sep	1955
13 46.8	V Kuts	USSR	Belgrade	18 Sep	1955
13 40.6	S Iharos	Hungary	Budapest	23 Oct	1955
13 36.8	G Pirie	GB	Bergen	19 Jun	1956
13 35.0	V Kuts	USSR	Rome	13 Oct	1957
13 34.8	R Clarke	Australia	Hobart	16 Jan	1965
13 33.6	R Clarke	Australia	Auckland	1 Feb	1965
13 25.8	R Clarke	Australia	Los Angeles	4 Jun	1965
13 24.2	K Keino	Kenya	Auckland	30 Nov	1965
13 16.6	R Clarke	Australia	Stockholm	5 Jul	1966
13 16.4	L Viren	Finland	Helsinki	14 Sep	1972
13 13.0	E Puttemans	Belgium	Brussels	20 Sep	1972
13 12.9	D Quax	NZ	Stockholm	5 Jul	1977
13 08.4	H Rono	Kenya	Berkeley	8 Apr	1978
13 06.20	H Rono	Kenya	Knarvik	13 Sep	1981
13 00.41	D Moorcroft	GB	Oslo	7 Jul	1982

10,000 metres

min sec

31 02.4	A Shrubb	GB	Glasgow	5 Nov	1904

30 58.8	J Bouin	France	Colombes	16 Nov	1911
30 40.2	P Nurmi	Finland	Stockholm	22 Jun	1921
30 35.4	V Ritola	Finland	Helsinki	25 May	1924
30 23.2	V Ritola	Finland	Colombes	6 Jul	1924
30 06.2	P Nurmi	Finland	Kuopio	31 Aug	1924
30 05.6	I Salminen	Finland	Kouvola	18 Jul	1937
30 02.0	T Maki	Finland	Tampere	29 Sep	1938
29 52.6	T Maki	Finland	Helsinki	17 Sep	1939
29 35.4	V Heino	Finland	Helsinki	25 Aug	1944
29 28.2	E Zátopek	Czech	Ostrava	11 Jun	1949
29 17.2	V Heino	Finland	Kouvola	1 Sep	1949
29 21.2	E Zátopek	Czech	Ostrava	22 Oct	1949
29 02.6	E Zátopek	Czech	Turku	4 Aug	1950
29 01.6	E Zátopek	Czech	Stara Boleslav	1 Nov	1953
28 54.2	E Zátopek	Czech	Brussels	1 Jun	1954
28 42.8	S Iharos	Hungary	Budapest	15 Jul	1956
28 30.4	V Kuts	USSR	Moscow	11 Sep	1956
28 18.8	P Bolotnikov	USSR	Kiev	15 Oct	1960
28 18.2	P Bolotnikov	USSR	Moscow	11 Aug	1962
28 15.6	R Clarke	Australia	Melbourne	18 Dec	1963
27 39.4	R Clarke	Australia	Oslo	14 Jul	1965
27 38.35	L Viren	Finland	Munich	3 Sep	1972
27 30.8	D Bedford	GB	London	13 Jul	1973
27 30.5	S Kimobwa	Kenya	Helsinki	30 Jun	1977
27 22.5	H Rono	Kenya	Vienna	11 Jun	1978

3,000 metres steeplechase

min sec

8 49.6	S Rozsnyói	Hungary	Berne	28 Aug	1954
8 47.8	P Karvonen	Finland	Helsinki	1 Jul	1955
8 45.4	P Karvonen	Finland	Oslo	15 Jul	1955
8 45.4	V Vlasyenko	USSR	Moscow	18 Aug	1955
8 41.2	J Chromik	Poland	Brünn	31 Aug	1955
8 40.2	J Chromik	Poland	Budapest	11 Sep	1955
8 39.8	S Rzhishchin	USSR	Moscow	14 Aug	1956
8 35.6	S Rozsnyói	Hungary	Budapest	16 Sep	1956
8 35.6	S Rzhishchin	USSR	Tallinn	21 Jul	1958
8 32.0	J Chromik	Poland	Warsaw	2 Aug	1958
8 31.4	Z Krzyszkowiak				
		Poland	Tula	26 Jun	1960
8 31.2	G Taran	USSR	Kiev	28 May	1961
8 30.4	Z Krzyszkowiak				
		Poland	Walcz	10 Aug	1961
8 29.6	G Roelants	Belgium	Louvain	7 Sep	1963
8 26.4	G Roelants	Belgium	Brussels	7 Aug	1965
8 24.2	J Kuha	Finland	Stockholm	17 Jul	1968
8 22.2	V Dudin	USSR	Kiev	19 Aug	1969
8 22.0	K O'Brien	Australia	Berlin	4 Jul	1970
8 20.8	A Gärderud	Sweden	Helsinki	14 Sep	1972
8 19.8	B Jipcho	Kenya	Helsinki	19 Jun	1973
8 14.0	B Jipcho	Kenya	Helsinki	27 Jun	1973

8 10.4	A Gärderud	Sweden	Oslo	25 Jun 1975
8 09.8	A Gärderud	Sweden	Stockholm	1 Jul 1975
8 08.0	A Gärderud	Sweden	Montreal	28 Jul 1976
8 05.4	H Rono	Kenya	Seattle	13 May 1978

110 metres hurdles

sec

15.0	F Smithson	US	London	25 Jul 1908
14.8	E Thomson	Canada	Philadelphia	29 May 1920
14.8	S Pettersson	Sweden	Stockholm	18 Sep 1927
14.6	G Weightman-Smith	US	Amsterdam	31 Jul 1928
14.4	E Wennstrom	Sweden	Stockholm	25 Aug 1929
14.4	B Sjostedt	Finland	Helsinki	5 Sep 1931
14.4	P Beard	US	Cambridge, US	18 Jun 1932
14.4	G Salin	US	Iowa City	25 Jun 1932
14.4	J Keller	US	Palo Alto	16 Jun 1932
14.4	G Salin	US	Los Angeles	2 Aug 1932
14.4	J Morriss	US	Budapest	12 Aug 1933
14.3	P Beard	US	Stockholm	26 Jul 1934
14.2	P Beard	US	Oslo	6 Aug 1934
14.2	A Moreau	US	Oslo	2 Aug 1935
14.1	F Towns	US	Chicago	19 Jun 1936
14.1	F Towns	US	Berlin	6 Aug 1936
13.7	F Towns	US	Oslo	27 Aug 1936
13.7	F Wolcott	US	Philadelphia	29 Jun 1941
13.6*	H Dillard	US	Lawrence	17 Apr 1948
13.5*	D Attlesey	US	Fresno	13 May 1950
13.6	D Attlesey	US	College Park, US	24 Jun 1950
13.5	D Attlesey	US	Helsinki	10 Jul 1950
13.4	J Davis	US	Bakersfield	22 Jun 1956
13.4*	J Davis	US	Bendigo	17 Nov 1956
13.2	M Lauer	West Germany	Zürich	7 Jul 1959
13.2	L Calhoun	US	Berne	21 Aug 1960
13.2	E McCullouch	US	Minneapolis	16 Jul 1967
13.2	W Davenport	US	Zürich	4 Jul 1969
13.0*	R Milburn	US	Eugene	25 Jun 1971
13.2	R Milburn	US	Munich	7 Sep 1972
13.0*	R Milburn	US	Eugene	20 Jun 1973
13.1	R Milburn	US	Zürich	6 Jul 1973
13.1	R Milburn	US	Siena	22 Jul 1973
13.1	G Drut	France	St Maur	23 Jul 1975
13.0	G Drut	France	Berlin	22 Aug 1975

Automatic Timing since 1 May 1977

13.24	R Milburn	US	Munich	7 Sep 1972
13.21	A Casañas	Cuba	Sofia	21 Aug 1977
13.16	R Nehemiah	US	San José	14 Apr 1979
13.00	R Nehemiah	US	Westwood	6 May 1979

| 12.93 | R Nehemiah | US | Zürich | 19 Aug 1981 |

* timed over 120 yards (109.73 metres)

400 metres hurdles

sec

55.0	C Bacon	US	London	22 Jul 1908
54.2	J Norton	US	Pasadena	26 Jun 1920
54.0	F Loomis	US	Antwerp	16 Aug 1920
53.8	S Pettersson	Sweden	Colombes	4 Oct 1925
54.2*	D Cecil Burghley	GB	London	2 Jul 1927
54.6*	J Gibson	US	Lincoln	2 Jul 1927
52.0	M Taylor	US	Philadelphia	4 Jul 1928
52.0	G Hardin	US	Los Angeles	1 Aug 1932
51.8	G Hardin	US	Milwaukee	30 Jun 1934
50.6	G Hardin	US	Stockholm	26 Jul 1934
50.4	Y Lituyev	USSR	Budapest	20 Sep 1953
49.5	G Davis	US	Los Angeles	29 Jun 1956
49.7*	G Potgieter	S Africa	Cardiff	22 Jul 1958
49.2	G Davis	US	Budapest	6 Aug 1958
49.3*	G Potgieter	S Africa	Bloemfontein	16 Apr 1960
49.2	S Morale	Italy	Belgrade	14 Sep 1962
49.1	W Cawley	US	Los Angeles	13 Sep 1964
48.1	G Vanderstock	US	Echo Summit	11 Sep 1968
48.1	D Hemery	GB	Mexico	15 Oct 1968
47.8	J Akii-Bua	Uganda	Munich	2 Sep 1972

Automatic Timing since 1 May 1977

47.82	J Akii-Bua	Uganda	Munich	2 Sep 1972
47.64	E Moses	US	Montreal	25 Jul 1976
47.45	E Moses	US	Westwood	11 Jun 1977
47.13	E Moses	US	Milan	3 Jul 1980
47.02	E Moses	US	Koblenz	31 Aug 1983

* timed over 440 yards (402.34 metres)

4×100 metres relay

sec

42.3	Germany		Stockholm	8 Jul 1912
42.2	United States		Antwerp	22 Aug 1920
42.4*	New York AC, US		Pasadena	5 Jul 1921
42.4*	Univ of Illinois, US		Des Moines	28 Apr 1923
42.0	Great Britain		Colombes	12 Jul 1924
42.0	Netherlands		Colombes	12 Jul 1924
41.0	United States		Colombes	13 Jul 1924
41.0*	Newark AC, US		Lincoln	4 Jul 1927
41.0	Eintracht Frankfurt, Germany		Halle	10 Jun 1928
41.0	United States		Amsterdam	5 Aug 1928
40.8	Germany		Berlin	2 Sep 1928
40.8	SC Charlottenburg, Germany		Breslau	22 Jul 1929

40.8*	Univ of S California, US	Fresno	9 May 1931
40.6	Germany	Kassel	14 Jun 1932
40.0	United States	Los Angeles	7 Aug 1932
39.8	United States	Berlin	9 Aug 1936
39.5	United States	Melbourne	1 Dec 1956
39.7*	Abilene Christian College, US	Modesto	31 May 1958
39.5	Germany	Cologne	29 Aug 1958
39.6*	Univ of Texas, US	Modesto	30 May 1959
39.5	Germany	Rome	7 Sep 1960
39.5	Germany	Rome	8 Sep 1960
39.1	United States	Moscow	15 Jul 1961
39.0	United States	Tokyo	21 Oct 1964
38.6*	Univ of S California, US	Provo	17 Jun 1967
38.6	Jamaica	Mexico	19 Oct 1968
38.3	Jamaica	Mexico	19 Oct 1968
38.2	United States	Mexico	20 Oct 1968
38.2	United States	Munich	10 Sep 1972
Automatic Timing since 1 May 1977			
38.19	United States	Munich	10 Sep 1972
38.03	United States	Düsseldorf	3 Sep 1977
37.86	United States	Helsinki	10 Aug 1983

* timed over 440 yards (402.34 metres)

4 × 400 metres relay

min sec

3 18.2	Irish-American AC, US	New York	4 Sep 1911
3 16.6	United States	Stockholm	15 Jul 1912
3 16.0	United States	Colombes	13 Jul 1924
3 14.2	United States	Amsterdam	5 Aug 1928
3 13.4	United States	London	11 Aug 1928
3 12.6	Stanford University, US	Fresno	8 May 1931
3 08.2	United States	Los Angeles	7 Aug 1932
3 03.9	Jamaica	Helsinki	27 Jul 1952
3 02.2	United States	Rome	8 Sep 1960
3 00.7	United States	Tokyo	21 Oct 1964
2 59.6	United States	Los Angeles	24 Jul 1966
2 56.16	United States	Mexico	20 Oct 1968

High jump

metres

2.00	G Horine	US	Palo Alto	18 May 1912
2.01	E Beeson	US	Berkeley	2 May 1914
2.03	H Osborn	US	Urbana	27 May 1924
2.04	W Marty	US	Fresno	13 May 1933
2.06	W Marty	US	Palo Alto	28 Apr 1934
2.07	C Johnson	US	New York	12 Jul 1936
2.07	D Albritton	US	New York	12 Jul 1936
2.09	M Walker	US	Malmo	12 Aug 1937

2.11	L Steers	US	Los Angeles	17 Jun	1941
2.12	W Davis	US	Dayton	27 Jun	1953
2.15	C Dumas	US	Los Angeles	29 Jun	1956
2.16	Y Styepanov	USSR	Leningrad	13 Jul	1957
2.17	J Thomas	US	Philadelphia	30 Apr	1960
2.17	J Thomas	US	Cambridge,US	21 May	1960
2.18	J Thomas	US	Bakersfield	24 Jun	1960
2.22	J Thomas	US	Palo Alto	1 Jul	1960
2.23	V Brumel	USSR	Moscow	18 Jun	1961
2.24	V Brumel	USSR	Moscow	16 Jul	1961
2.25	V Brumel	USSR	Sofia	31 Aug	1961
2.26	V Brumel	USSR	Palo Alto	22 Jul	1962
2.27	V Brumel	USSR	Moscow	29 Jul	1962
2.28	V Brumel	USSR	Moscow	21 Jul	1963
2.29	P Matzdorf	US	Berkeley	3 Jul	1971
2.30	D Stones	US	Munich	11 Jul	1973
2.31	D Stones	US	Philadelphia	5 Jun	1976
2.32	D Stones	US	Philadelphia	4 Aug	1976
2.33	V Yashchenko	USSR	Richmond	3 Jul	1977
2.34	V Yashchenko	USSR	Tbilisi	16 Jun	1976
2.35	J Wszola	Poland	Eberstadt	25 May	1980
2.35	D Mogenburg	West Germany	Rehlingen	26 May	1980
2.36	G Wessig	East Germany	Moscow	1 Aug	1980
2.37	Z Jianhua	China	Peking	11 Jun	1983
2.38	Z Jianhua	China	Shanghai	22 Sep	1983

Pole vault

metres

4.02	M Wright	US	Cambridge,US	8 Jun	1912
4.09	F Foss	US	Antwerp	20 Aug	1920
4.12	C Hoff	Norway	Copenhagen	3 Sep	1922
4.21	C Hoff	Norway	Copenhagen	22 Jul	1923
4.23	C Hoff	Norway	Oslo	13 Aug	1925
4.25	C Hoff	Norway	Turku	27 Sep	1925
4.26	S Carr	US	Philadelphia	28 May	1927
4.30	L Barnes	US	Fresno	28 Apr	1928
4.37	B Graber	US	Palo Alto	16 Jul	1932
4.39	K Brown	US	Cambridge,US	1 Jun	1935
4.43	G Varoff	US	Princeton	4 Jul	1936
4.54	B Sefton	US	Los Angeles	29 May	1937
4.54	E Meadows	US	Los Angeles	29 May	1937
4.60	C Warmerdam	US	Fresno	29 Jun	1940
4.72	C Warmerdam	US	Compton	6 Jun	1941
4.77	C Warmerdam	US	Modesto	23 May	1942
4.78	B Gutowski	US	Palo Alto	27 Apr	1957
4.80	D Bragg	US	Palo Alto	2 Jul	1960
4.83	G Davies	US	Boulder	20 May	1961
4.89	J Uelses	US	Santa Barbara	31 Mar	1962

4.93	D Tork	US	Walnut	28 Apr 1962
4.94	P Nikula	Finland	Kauhava	22 Jun 1962
5.00	B Sternberg	US	Philadelphia	27 Apr 1963
5.08	B Sternberg	US	Compton	7 Jun 1963
5.13	J Pennel	US	London	5 Aug 1963
5.20	J Pennel	US	Coral Gables	24 Aug 1963
5.23	F Hansen	US	San Diego	13 Jun 1964
5.28	F Hansen	US	Los Angeles	25 Jul 1964
5.32	B Seagren	US	Fresno	14 May 1966
5.34	J Pennel	US	Los Angeles	23 Jul 1966
5.36	B Seagren	US	San Diego	10 Jun 1967
5.38	P Wilson	US	Bakersfield	23 Jun 1967
5.41	B Seagren	US	Echo Summit	12 Sep 1968
5.44	J Pennel	US	Sacramento	21 Jun 1969
5.45	W Nordwig	East Germany	Berlin	17 Jun 1970
5.46	W Nordwig	East Germany	Turin	3 Sep 1970
5.49	C Papanicolaou	Greece	Athens	24 Oct 1970
5.51	K Isaksson	Sweden	Austin	8 Apr 1972
5.54	K Isaksson	Sweden	Los Angeles	15 Apr 1972
5.55	K Isaksson	Sweden	Helsingborg	12 Jun 1972
5.63	B Seagren	US	Eugene	2 Jul 1972
5.65	D Roberts	US	Gainesville	28 Mar 1975
5.67	E Bell	US	Wichita	29 May 1976
5.70	D Roberts	US	Eugene	22 Jun 1976
5.72	W Kozakiewicz	Poland	Milan	11 May 1980
5.75	T Vigneron	France	Colombes	1 Jun 1980
5.75	T Vigneron	France	Lille	29 Jun 1980
5.77	P Houvion	France	Paris	17 Jul 1980
5.78	W Kozakiewicz	Poland	Moscow	30 Jul 1980
5.80	T Vigneron	France	Mâcon	20 Jun 1981
5.81	V Polyakov	USSR	Tbilisi	26 Jun 1981
5.82	P Quinon	France	Cologne	28 Aug 1983
5.83	T Vigneron	France	Rome	1 Sep 1983

Long jump

metres

7.61	P O'Connor	Ireland	Dublin	5 Aug 1901
7.69	E Gourdin	US	Cambridge, US	23 Jul 1921
7.76	R LeGendre	US	Colombes	7 Jul 1924
7.89	W DeHart Hubbard	US	Chicago	13 Jun 1925
7.90	E Hamm	US	Cambridge, US	7 Jul 1928
7.93	S Cator	Haiti	Colombes	9 Sep 1928
7.98	C Nambu	Japan	Tokyo	27 Oct 1931
8.13	J Owens	US	Ann Arbor	25 May 1935
8.21	R Boston	US	Walnut	12 Aug 1960
8.24	R Boston	US	Modesto	27 May 1961
8.28	R Boston	US	Moscow	16 Jul 1961

8.31	I Ter-Ovanesyan	USSR	Yerevan	10 Jun 1962
8.31	R Boston	US	Kingston	15 Aug 1964
8.34	R Boston	US	Los Angeles	12 Sep 1964
8.35	R Boston	US	Modesto	29 May 1965
8.35	I Ter-Ovanesyan	USSR	Mexico	19 Oct 1967
8.90	B Beamon	US	Mexico	18 Oct 1968

Triple jump

metres

15.52	D Ahearne	US	New York	30 May 1911
15.52	A Winter	Australia	Colombes	12 Jul 1924
15.58	M Oda	Japan	Tokyo	27 Oct 1931
15.72	C Nambu	Japan	Los Angeles	4 Aug 1932
15.78	J Metcalfe	Australia	Sydney	14 Dec 1935
16.00	N Tajima	Japan	Berlin	6 Aug 1936
16.00	AF da Silva	Brazil	São Paulo	3 Dec 1950
16.01	AF da Silva	Brazil	Rio de Janeiro	3 Sep 1951
16.12	AF da Silva	Brazil	Helsinki	23 Jul 1952
16.22	AF da Silva	Brazil	Helsinki	23 Jul 1952
16.23	L Scherbakov	USSR	Moscow	19 Jul 1953
16.56	AF da Silva	Brazil	Mexico	16 Mar 1955
16.59	O Ryakhovskiy	USSR	Moscow	28 Jul 1958
16.70	O Fedosyeyev	USSR	Nalchik	3 May 1959
17.03	J Schmidt	Poland	Olsztyn	5 Aug 1960
17.10	G Gentile	Italy	Mexico	16 Oct 1968
17.22	G Gentile	Italy	Mexico	17 Oct 1968
17.23	V Sanyeyev	USSR	Mexico	17 Oct 1968
17.27	N Prudencio	Brazil	Mexico	17 Oct 1968
17.39	V Sanyeyev	USSR	Mexico	17 Oct 1968
17.40	P Pérez	Cuba	Cali	5 Aug 1971
17.44	V Sanyeyev	USSR	Sukhumi	17 Oct 1972
17.89	JC de Oliveira	Brazil	Mexico	15 Oct 1975

Shot

metres

15.54	R Rose	US	San Francisco	21 Aug 1909
15.79	E Hirschfeld	Germany	Breslau	6 May 1928
15.87	J Kuck	US	Amsterdam	29 Jul 1928
16.04	E Hirschfeld	Germany	Bochum	26 Aug 1928
16.04	F Douda	Czech	Brünn	4 Oct 1931
16.05	Z Heljasz	Poland	Posnań	29 Jun 1932
16.16	L Sexton	US	Freeport	27 Aug 1932
16.20	F Douda	Czech	Prague	24 Sep 1932
16.48	J Lyman	US	Palo Alto	21 Apr 1934
16.80	J Torrance	US	Des Moines	27 Apr 1934
16.89	J Torrance	US	Milwaukee	30 June 1934
17.40	J Torrance	US	Oslo	5 Aug 1934
17.68	C Fonville	US	Lawrence	17 Apr 1948

17.79	J Fuchs	US	Oslo	28 Jul 1949
17.82	J Fuchs	US	Los Angeles	29 Apr 1950
17.90	J Fuchs	US	Visby	20 Aug 1950
17.95	J Fuchs	US	Eskilstuna	22 Aug 1950
18.00	P O'Brien	US	Fresno	9 May 1953
18.04	P O'Brien	US	Compton	5 Jun 1953
18.42	P O'Brien	US	Los Angeles	8 May 1954
18.43	P O'Brien	US	Los Angeles	21 May 1954
18.54	P O'Brien	US	Los Angeles	11 Jun 1954
18.62	P O'Brien	US	Salt Lake City	5 May 1956
18.69	P O'Brien	US	Los Angeles	15 Jun 1956
19.06	P O'Brien	US	Eugene	3 Sep 1956
19.25	P O'Brien	US	Los Angeles	1 Nov 1956
19.25	D Long	US	Santa Barbara	28 Mar 1959
19.30	P O'Brien	US	Albuquerque	1 Aug 1959
19.38	D Long	US	Los Angeles	5 Mar 1960
19.45	B Nieder	US	Palo Alto	19 Mar 1960
19.67	D Long	US	Los Angeles	26 Mar 1960
19.99	B Nieder	US	Austin	2 Apr 1960
20.06	B Nieder	US	Walnut	12 Aug 1960
20.08	D Long	US	Los Angeles	18 May 1962
20.10	D Long	US	Los Angeles	4 Apr 1964
20.20	D Long	US	Los Angeles	29 May 1964
20.68	D Long	US	Los Angeles	25 Jul 1964
21.52	R Matson	US	College Station	8 May 1965
21.78	R Matson	US	College Station	22 Apr 1967
21.82	A Feuerbach	US	San José	5 May 1973
21.85	T Albritton	US	Honolulu	21 Feb 1976
22.00	A Barishnikov	USSR	Colombes	10 Jul 1976
22.15	U Beyer	E Germany	Gothenburg	6 Jul 1978
22.22	U Beyer	E Germany	Los Angeles	26 Jun 1983

Discus

metres

47.58	J Duncan	US	New York	27 May 1912
47.61	T Lieb	US	Chicago	14 Sep 1924
47.89	G Hartranft	US	San Francisco	2 May 1925
48.20	C Houser	US	Palo Alto	3 Apr 1926
49.90	E Krenz	US	Palo Alto	9 Mar 1929
51.03	E Krenz	US	Palo Alto	17 May 1930
51.73	P Jessup	US	Pittsburgh	23 Aug 1930
52.42	H Andersson	Sweden	Oslo	25 Aug 1934
53.10	W Schroder	Germany	Magdeburg	28 Apr 1935
53.26	A Harris	US	Palo Alto	20 Jun 1941
53.34	A Consolini	Italy	Milan	26 Oct 1941
54.23	A Consolini	Italy	Milan	14 Apr 1946
54.93	B Fitch	US	Minneapolis	8 Jun 1946
55.33	A Consolini	Italy	Milan	10 Oct 1948

56.46	F Gordien	US	Lisbon	9 Jul 1949
56.97	F Gordien	US	Hameenlinna	14 Aug 1949
57.93	S Iness	US	Lincoln	20 Jun 1953
58.10	F Gordien	US	Pasadena	11 Jul 1953
59.28	F Gordien	US	Pasadena	22 Aug 1953
59.91	E Piatkowski	Poland	Warsaw	14 Jun 1959
59.91	R Babka	US	Walnut	12 Aug 1960
60.56	J Silvester	US	Frankfurt	11 Aug 1961
60.72	J Silvester	US	Brussels	20 Aug 1961
61.10	A Oerter	US	Los Angeles	18 May 1962
61.64	V Trusenyov	USSR	Leningrad	4 Jun 1962
62.45	A Oerter	US	Chicago	1 Jul 1962
62.62	A Oerter	US	Walnut	27 Apr 1963
62.94	A Oerter	US	Walnut	25 Apr 1964
64.55	L Danek	Czech	Turnov	2 Aug 1964
65.22	L Danek	Czech	Sokolov	12 Oct 1965
66.54	J Silvester	US	Modesto	25 May 1968
68.40	J Silvester	US	Reno	18 Sep 1968
68.40	R Bruch	Sweden	Stockholm	5 Jul 1972
68.48	J van Reenen	S Africa	Stellenbosch	14 Mar 1975
69.08	J Powell	US	Long Beach	4 May 1975
69.18	M Wilkins	US	Walnut	24 Apr 1976
69.80	M Wilkins	US	San José	1 May 1976
70.24	M Wilkins	US	San José	1 May 1976
70.86	M Wilkins	US	San José	1 May 1976
71.16	W Schmidt	E Germany	Berlin	9 Aug 1978
71.86	Y Dumtchev	USSR	Moscow	29 May 1983

Hammer

metres

57.77	P Ryan	US	New York	17 Aug 1913
59.00	E Blask	Germany	Stockholm	27 Aug 1938
59.02	I Németh	Hungary	Tata	14 Jul 1948
59.57	I Németh	Hungary	Katowice	4 Sep 1949
59.88	I Németh	Hungary	Budapest	19 May 1950
60.34	J Csermak	Hungary	Helsinki	24 Jul 1952
61.25	S Strandli	Norway	Oslo	14 Sep 1952
62.36	S Strandli	Norway	Oslo	5 Sep 1953
63.34	M Krivonosov	USSR	Bern	29 Aug 1954
64.05	S Nyenashev	USSR	Baku	12 Dec 1954
64.33	M Krivonosov	USSR	Warsaw	4 Aug 1955
64.52	M Krivonosov	USSR	Belgrade	19 Jul 1955
65.85	M Krivonosov	USSR	Nalchik	25 Apr 1956
66.38	M Krivonosov	USSR	Minsk	8 Jul 1956
67.32	M Krivonosov	USSR	Tashkent	22 Oct 1956
68.54	H Connolly	US	Los Angeles	2 Nov 1956
68.68	H Connolly	US	Bakersfield	20 Jun 1958
70.33	H Connolly	US	Walnut	12 Aug 1960
70.67	H Connolly	US	Palo Alto	21 Jul 1962

71.06	H Connolly	US	Ceres	29 May 1965
71.26	H Connolly	US	Walnut	20 Jun 1965
73.74	G Zsivótzky	Hungary	Debrecen	4 Sep 1965
73.76	G Zsivótzky	Hungary	Budapest	14 Sep 1968
74.52	R Klim	USSR	Budapest	15 Jun 1969
74.68	A Bondarchuk	USSR	Athens	20 Sep 1969
75.48	A Bondarchuk	USSR	Rovno	12 Oct 1969
76.40	W Schmidt	W Germany	Lahr	4 Sep 1971
76.60	R Theimer	E Germany	Leipzig	4 Jul 1974
76.66	A Spiridonov	USSR	Munich	11 Sep 1974
76.70	K Riehm	W Germany	Rehlingen	19 May 1975
77.56	K Riehm	W Germany	Rehlingen	19 May 1975
78.50	K Riehm	W Germany	Rehlingen	19 May 1975
79.30	W Schmidt	W Germany	Frankfurt	14 Aug 1975
80.14	B Zaichuk	USSR	Moscow	9 Jul 1978
80.32	K Riehm	W Germany	Heidenheim	6 Aug 1978
80.38	Y Syedikh	USSR	Leselidze	16 May 1980
80.46	J Tamm	USSR	Leselidze	16 May 1980
80.64	Y Syedikh	USSR	Leselidze	16 May 1980
81.66	S Litvinov	USSR	Sochi	24 May 1980
81.80	Y Syedikh	USSR	Moscow	31 Jul 1980
83.98	S Litvinov	USSR	Moscow	4 Jun 1982
84.14	S Litvinov	USSR	Moscow	21 Jun 1983

Javelin

metres

62.32	E Lemming	Sweden	Stockholm	29 Sep 1912
66.10	J Myyra	Finland	Stockholm	25 Aug 1919
66.62	G Lindstrom	Sweden	Eksjo	12 Oct 1924
69.88	E Penttila	Finland	Viipuri	8 Oct 1927
71.01	E Lundqvist	Sweden	Stockholm	15 Aug 1928
71.57	M Järvinen	Finland	Viipuri	8 Aug 1930
71.70	M Järvinen	Finland	Tampere	17 Aug 1930
71.88	M Järvinen	Finland	Vaasa	31 Aug 1930
72.93	M Järvinen	Finland	Viipuri	14 Sep 1930
74.02	M Järvinen	Finland	Turku	27 Jun 1932
74.28	M Järvinen	Finland	Mikkeli	25 May 1933
74.61	M Järvinen	Finland	Vaasa	7 Jun 1933
76.10	M Järvinen	Finland	Helsinki	15 Jun 1933
76.66	M Järvinen	Finland	Turin	7 Sep 1934
77.23	M Järvinen	Finland	Helsinki	18 Jun 1936
77.87	Y Nikkanen	Finland	Karhila	25 Aug 1938
78.70	Y Nikkanen	Finland	Kotka	16 Oct 1938
80.41	F Held	US	Pasadena	8 Aug 1953
81.75	F Held	US	Modesto	21 May 1955
83.56	S Nikkinen	Finland	Kuhmoinen	24 Jun 1956
83.66	J Sidlo	Poland	Milan	30 Jun 1956
85.71	E Danielsen	Norway	Melbourne	26 Nov 1956
86.04	A Cantello	US	Compton	5 Jun 1959

86.74	C Lievore	Italy	Milan	1 Jun 1961
87.12	T Pedersen	Norway	Oslo	1 Jul 1964
91.72	T Pedersen	Norway	Oslo	2 Sep 1964
91.98	J Lusis	USSR	Saarijarvi	23 Jun 1968
92.70	J Kinnunen	Finland	Tampere	18 Jun 1969
93.80	J Lusis	USSR	Stockholm	6 Jul 1972
94.08	K Wolfermann	W Germany	Leverkusen	5 May 1973
94.58	M Németh	Hungary	Montreal	26 Jul 1976
96.72	F Paragi	Hungary	Tata	23 Apr 1980
99.72	T Petranoff	US	Los Angeles	14 May 1983

Ron Clarke (Australia) who was a prolific record-breaker in the mid 1960's.

Bob Beamon's (USA) giant leap of 8.90 metres to win Olympic gold in Mexico.

Decathlon

100 metres	long jump	shot	high jump	400 metres
1920 tables	**1962 tables**			
7481.69	**6270**	**A Klumberg**	**Estonia**	
12.3	6.59	12.92	1.75	55.0
7710.775	**6668**	**H Osborn**	**US**	
11.2	6.92	11.435	1.97	53.2
7832.03	**6651**	**P Yrjola**	**Finland**	
11.8	6.54	13.93	1.85	52.4
8018.99	**6768**	**P Yrjola**	**Finland**	
11.7	6.73	14.27	1.85	52.8
8053.29	**6774**	**P Yrjola**	**Finland**	
11.8	6.72	14.11	1.87	53.2
8117.300	**6867**	**P Yrjola**	**Finland**	
11.6	6.76	14.72	1.85	53.2
8255.475	**7036**	**A Järvinen**	**Finland**	
11.1	6.89	13.14	1.80	50.0
8462.235	**6896**	**J Bausch**	**US**	
11.7	6.95	15.32	1.70	54.2
8467.620	**6999**	**H-H Sievert**	**Germany**	
11.4	7.09	14.55	1.825	54.0
8790.460	**7292**	**H-H Sievert**	**Germany**	
11.1	7.48	15.31	1.80	52.2
1934 tables	**1962 tables**			
7883	**7394**	**G Morris**	**US**	
10.7	6.86	14.45	1.87	50.7
7900	**7421**	**G Morris**	**US**	
11.1	6.97	14.10	1.85	49.4
8042	**7453**	**B Mathias**	**US**	
10.9	7.09	14.48	1.85	51.0
1950 tables	**1962/77 tables**			
	7690	**B Mathias**	**US**	
10.8	7.15	15.21	1.89	50.8
7887	**7731**	**B Mathias**	**US**	
10.9	6.98	15.30	1.90	50.2
7985	**7758**	**R Johnson**	**US**	
10.5	7.49	13.80	1.85	49.7
8014	**7760**	**V Kuznyetsov**	**USSR**	
11.0	7.30	14.49	1.75	49.1
8302	**7896**	**R Johnson**	**US**	
10.6	7.17	14.69	1.80	48.2
8357	**7957**	**V Kusnyetsov**	**USSR**	
10.7	7.35	14.68	1.89	49.2
8683	**8063**	**R Johnson**	**US**	
10.5	7.55	15.85	1.78	48.6
	8089	**Y Chuan-Kwang**	**Taiwan**	
10.7	7.17	13.22	1.92	47.7

110 metres hurdles	discus	pole vault	javelin	1,500 metres
	Helsinki			**16/17 Sep 1922**
17.0	39.64	3.40	62.20	5 11.3
	Colombes			**11/12 Jul 1924**
16.0	34.51	3.50	46.69	4 50.0
	Viipuri			**17/18 Jul 1926**
16.9	37.31	3.30	56.70	4 41.1
	Helsinki			**16/17 Jul 1927**
16.8	40.76	3.20	57.40	4 41.8
	Amsterdam			**3/4 Aug 1928**
16.6	42.09	3.30	55.70	4 44.0
	Aalborg			**9/10 Jul 1930**
16.1	39.66	3.10	58.88	4 37.5
	Viipuri			**19/20 Jul 1930**
15.4	36.47	3.60	58.15	4 54.2
	Los Angeles			**5/6 Aug.1932**
16.2	44.58	4.00	61.91	5 17.0
	Hamburg			**22/23 Jul 1933**
16.2	46.66	3.40	59.58	4 59.8
	Hamburg			**7/8 Jul 1934**
15.8	47.23	3.43	58.32	4 58.8
	Milwaukee			**26/27 Jun 1936**
14.9	43.11	3.45	56.06	4 48.2
	Berlin			**7/8 Aug 1936**
14.9	43.02	3.50	54.52	4 33.2
	Tulare			**29/30 Jun 1950**
14.7	44.62	3.98	55.59	5 05.1
	Tulare			**1/2 Jul 1952**
14.6	48.15	3.75	59.09	4 55.3
	Helsinki			**25/26 Jul 1952**
14.7	46.89	4.00	59.21	4 50.8
	Kingsburg			**10/11 Jun 1955**
14.5	47.20	3.87	59.09	5 01.5
	Krasnodar			**17/18 May 1958**
14.5	47.50	4.00	66.16	4 50.0
	Moscow			**27/28 Jul 1958**
14.9	49.06	3.95	72.59	5 05.0
	Moscow			**16/17 May 1959**
14.7	49.94	4.20	65.06	5 04.6
	Eugene			**8/9 Jul 1960**
14.5	51.98	3.97	71.09	5 09.9
	Walnut			**27/28 Apr 1963**
14.0	40.99	4.84	71.75	5 02.4

Decathlon cont.

100 metres	long jump	shot		high jump		400 metres
	8230	**R Hodge**		**US**		
10.5	7.51	17.25		1.85		48.9
	8319	**K Bendlin**		**W Germany**		
10.6	7.55	14.50		1.84		47.9
	8417	**B Toomey**		**US**		
10.3	7.76	14.38		1.93		47.1
	8454/8456	**N Avilov**		**USSR**		
11.00	7.68	14.36		2.12		48.45
	8524	**B Jenner**		**US**		
10.7	7.17	15.25		2.01		48.7
	8538	**B Jenner**		**US**		
10.7	7.19	14.04		2.00		48.6
	8618/8617	**B Jenner**		**US**		
10.94	7.22	15.35		2.03		47.51
	8622	**D Thompson**		**GB**		
10.55	7.72	14.46		2.11		48.04
	8649	**G Kratschmer**		**W Germany**		
10.58	7.80	15.47		2.00		48.04
	8704	**D Thompson**		**GB**		
10.50	7.95	15.31		2.08		46.86
	8723	**J Hingsen**		**W Germany**		
10.74	7.85	16.00		2.15		47.65
	8743	**D Thompson**		**GB**		
10.51	7.80	15.44		2.03		47.11
	8777	**J Hingsen**		**W Germany**		
10.92	7.74	15.94		2.15		47.90

20,000 metres walk

hr m sec

1 39 22.0 N Petersen	Denmark	Copenhagen	30 Jun 1918
1 39 20.4 A Valente	Italy	Bologna	2 Dec 1926
1 38 53.2 A Callegari	Italy	Milan	26 Dec 1926
1 37 42.2 D Pavesi	Italy	Milan	23 Oct 1927
1 36 34.4 A Valente	Italy	Genoa	25 Oct 1930
1 34 26.0 J Dalins	Latvia	Riga	1 Jun 1933
1 32 28.4 J Mikaelsson	Sweden	Vaxjo	12 Jul 1942
1 30 26.4 J Dolezal	Czech	Stara Boleslav	1 Nov 1953
1 30 02.8 V Golubnichiy	USSR	Kiev	2 Oct 1955
1 28 45.2 L Sprin	USSR	Kiev	13 Jun 1956
1 27 58.2 M Lavrov	USSR	Moscow	13 Aug 1956
1 27 38.6 G Panichkin	USSR	Stalingrad	9 May 1958
1 27 05.0 V Golubnichiy	USSR	Simferopol	23 Sep 1958

110 metres hurdles	discus	pole vault	javelin	1,500 metres
	Los Angeles			**23/24 Jul 1966**
15.2	50.44	4.10	64.49	4 40.4
	Heidelberg			**13/14 May 1967**
14.8	46.31	4.10	74.85	4 19.4
	Los Angeles			**10/11 Dec 1969**
14.3	46.49	4.27	65.74	4 39.4
	Munich			**7/8 Sep 1972**
14.31	46.98	4.55	61.66	4 22.8
	Eugene			**9/10 Aug 1975**
14.6	50.00	4.70	65.52	4 16.6
	Eugene			**25/26 Jun 1976**
14.3	51.68	4.60	69.28	4 16.4
	Montreal			**29/30 Jul 1976**
14.84	50.04	4.80	68.52	4 12.61
	Gotzis			**17/18 May 1980**
14.37	42.98	4.90	65.38	4 25.49
	Bernhausen			**13/14 Jun 1980**
13.92	45.52	4.60	66.50	4 24.15
	Gotzis			**22/23 May 1982**
14.31	44.34	4.90	60.52	4 30.55
	Ulm			**14/15 Aug 1982**
14.64	44.92	4.60	63.10	4 15.13
	Athens			**7/8 Sep 1982**
14.39	45.48	5.00	63.56	4 23.80
	Bernhausen			**4/5 Jun 1983**
14.11	46.80	14.70	77.26	4 19.76

1 26 45.8 G Agapov	USSR	Simferopol		4 Apr 1969
1 25 50.0 P Frenkel	E Germany	Erfurt		4 Jul 1970
1 25 19.4 P Frenkel	E Germany	Erfurt		24 Jun 1972
1 25 19.4 H-G Reimann	E Germany	Erfurt		24 Jun 1972
1 24 45.0 B Kannenberg	West Germany	Hamburg		25 May 1974
1 23 31.9 D Bautista	Mexico	Fana		14 May 1977
1 22 59.4 A Solomin	USSR	Alushta		26 Apr 1979
1 22 19.4 G Lélièvre	France	Epinay-sur-Seine		29 Apr 1979
1 20 58.6 D Colin	Mexico	Fana		26 May 1979
1 20 06.8 D Bautista	Mexico	Montreal		17 Oct 1979

50,000 metres walk

hr m sec

4 34 03.0 P Sievert	Germany	Munich	5 Oct 1924

4 32 52.0	J Ljunggren	Sweden	Gislaved	29 Jul 1951
4 31 21.6	A Róka	Hungary	Budapest	1 Jun 1952
4 29 58.0	J Ljunggren	Sweden	Fristad	8 Aug 1953
4 27 28.4	L Moc	Czech	Znojmo	13 Nov 1955
4 26 05.2	M Skront	Czech	Krnov	30 Apr 1956
4 21 07.0	L Moc	Czech	Prague	21 Jun 1956
4 16 08.6	S Lobastov	USSR	Moscow	23 Aug 1958
4 14 02.4	A Pamich	Italy	Rome	19 Nov 1961
4 10 51.8	C Hohne	E Germany	Potsdam	16 May 1965
4 08 05.0	C Hohne	E Germany	Berlin	18 Oct 1969
4 04 19.8	P Selzer	E Germany	Nürnberg	3 Oct 1971
4 03 42.6	V Soldatyenko	USSR	Moscow	5 Oct 1972
4 00 27.2	G Weidner	West Germany	Hamburg	8 Apr 1973
3 56 51.4	B Kannenberg	West Germany	Nerviano	16 Nov 1975
3 52 23.5	R Gonzales	Mexico	Førde	19 May 1978
3 41 39.0	R Gonzales	Mexico	Fana	25 May 1979

WOMEN

100 metres

sec

11.7	S Walasiewicz	Poland	Warsaw	26 Aug 1934
11.6	S Walasiewicz	Poland	Berlin	1 Aug 1937
11.5	F Blankers-Koen	Netherlands	Amsterdam	13 Jun 1948
11.5	M Jackson	Australia	Helsinki	22 Jul 1952
11.4	M Jackson	Australia	Gifu	4 Oct 1952
11.3	S Strickland	Australia	Warsaw	4 Aug 1955
11.3	V Krepkina	USSR	Kiev	13 Sep 1958
11.3	W Rudolph	US	Rome	2 Sep 1960
11.2	W Rudolph	US	Stuttgart	19 Jul 1961
11.2	W Tyus	US	Tokyo	15 Oct 1964
11.1	I Kirszenstein	Poland	Prague	9 Jul 1965
11.1	W Tyus	US	Kiev	31 Jul 1965
11.1	B Ferrell	US	Santa Barbara	2 Jul 1967
11.1	L Samotyosova	USSR	Leninakan	15 Aug 1968
11.1	I Kirszenstein-Szewinska	Poland	Mexico	14 Oct 1968
11.0	W Tyus	US	Mexico	15 Oct 1968
11.0	C Chi	Taiwan	Vienna	18 Jul 1970
11.0	R Meissner	E Germany	Berlin	2 Aug 1970
11.0	R Meissner-Stecher	E Germany	Berlin	31 Jul 1971
11.0	R Meissner-Stecher	E Germany	Potsdam	3 Jun 1972
11.0	E Stropahl	E Germany	Potsdam	15 Jun 1972

11.0	E Glesková	Czech	Budapest	1 Jul	1972
10.9	R Meissner-Stecher	E Germany	Ostrava	7 Jun	1973
10.8	R Meissner-Stecher	E Germany	Dresden	20 Jul	1973

Automatic Timing since 1 May 1977

11.08	W Tyus	US	Mexico	15 Oct	1968
11.07	R Meissner-Stecher	E Germany	Munich	2 Sep	1972
11.04	I Helten	W Germany	Fürth	13 Jun	1976
11.01	A Richter	W Germany	Montreal	25 Jul	1976
10.88	M Oelsner	E Germany	Dresden	1 Jul	1977
10.88	M Göhr	E Germany	Karl-Marx-Stadt	9 Jul	1982
10.81	M Göhr	E Germany	E Berlin	8 Jun	1983
10.79	E Ashford	US	Colorado Springs	3 Jul	1983

200 metres

sec

23.6	S Walasiewicz	Poland	Warsaw	15 Aug	1935
23.6	M Jackson	Australia	Helsinki	25 Jul	1952
23.4	M Jackson	Australia	Helsinki	25 Jul	1952
23.2	B Cuthbert	Australia	Sydney	16 Sep	1956
23.2*	B Cuthbert	Australia	Hobart	7 Mar	1960
22.9	W Rudolph	US	Corpus Christi	9 Jul	1960
22.9*	M Burvill	Australia	Perth	22 Feb	1964
22.7	I Kirszenstein	Poland	Warsaw	8 Aug	1965
22.5	I Kirszenstein-Szewinska	Poland	Mexico	18 Oct	1968
22.6*	C Chi	Taiwan	Los Angeles	3 Jul	1970
22.4	C Chi	Taiwan	Munich	12 Jul	1970
22.4	R Meissner-Stecher	E Germany	Munich	7 Sep	1972
22.1	R Meissner-Stecher	E Germany	Dresden	21 Jul	1973

Automatic Timing since 1 May 1977

22.21	I Kirszenstein-Szewinska	Poland	Potsdam	13 Jun	1974
22.06	M Koch	E Germany	Erfurt	28 May	1978
22.02	M Koch	E Germany	Leipzig	3 Jun	1979
21.71	M Koch	E Germany	Karl-Marx-Stadt	10 Jun	1979

* timed over 220 yards (201.36 metres)

400 metres

sec

57.0	M Matthews	Australia	Sydney	6 Jan	1957
57.0	M Chamberlain	N Zealand	Christchurch	16 Feb	1957

56.3	N Boyle	Australia	Sydney	24 Feb 1957
54.0	M Itkina	USSR	Minsk	8 Jun 1957
53.6	M Itkina	USSR	Moscow	6 Jul 1957
53.4	M Itkina	USSR	Krasnodar	12 Sep 1959
53.4	M Itkina	USSR	Belgrade	14 Sep 1962
51.9	S Keum Dan	N Korea	Pyongyang	23 Oct 1962
51.7	N Duclos	France	Athens	18 Sep 1969
51.7	C Besson	France	Athens	18 Sep 1969
51.0	M Neufville	Jamaica	Edinburgh	25 Jul 1970
51.0	M Zehrt	E Germany	Colombes	4 Jul 1972
49.9	I Kirszenstein-Szewinska	Poland	Warsaw	22 Jun 1974

Automatic Timing since 1 May 1977

50.14	R Salin	Finland	Rome	4 Sep 1974
49.77	C Brehmer	E Germany	Dresden	9 May 1976
49.75	I Kirszenstein-Szewinska	Poland	Bydgoszcz	22 Jun 1976
49.29	I Kirszenstein-Szewinska	Poland	Montreal	29 Jul 1976
49.19	M Koch	E Germany	Leipzig	2 Jul 1978
49.03	M Koch	E Germany	Potsdam	19 Aug 1978
48.94	M Koch	E Germany	Prague	31 Aug 1978
48.89	M Koch	E Germany	Potsdam	29 Jul 1979
48.60	M Koch	E Germany	Turin	4 Aug 1979
48.16	M Koch	E Germany	Athens	8 Sep 1982
47.99	J Kratochvilova	Czech	Helsinki	10 Aug 1983

800 metres

min sec

2 16.8	L Batschauer-Radke	Germany	Amsterdam	2 Aug 1928
2 15.9	A Larsson	Sweden	Stockholm	28 Aug 1944
2 14.8	A Larsson	Sweden	Helsingborg	19 Aug 1945
2 13.8	A Larsson	Sweden	Stockholm	30 Aug 1945
2 13.0	Y Vasilyeva	USSR	Moscow	17 Jul 1950
2 12.2	V Pomogayeva	USSR	Moscow	26 Jul 1951
2 12.0	N Pletnyova	USSR	Minsk	26 Aug 1951
2 08.5	N Pletnyova	USSR	Kiev	15 Jun 1952
2 07.3	N Pletnyova-Otkalenko	USSR	Moscow	27 Aug 1953
2 06.6	N Pletnyova-Otkalenko	USSR	Kiev	16 Sep 1954
2 05.0	N Pletnyova-Otkalenko	USSR	Zagreb	24 Sep 1955
2 04.3	L Shevtsova	USSR	Moscow	3 Jul 1960
2 04.3	L Shevtsova	USSR	Rome	7 Sep 1960
2 01.2	D Willis	Australia	Perth	3 Mar 1962
2 01.1	A Packer	GB	Tokyo	20 Oct 1964
2 01.0	J Pollock	Australia	Helsinki	28 Jun 1967
2 00.5	V Nikolić	Yugoslavia	London	20 Jul 1968

1 58.5	H Falck	W Germany	Stuttgart	11 Jul 1971
1 57.5	S Zlateva	Bulgaria	Athens	24 Aug 1973
1 56.0	V Gerasimova	USSR	Kiev	12 Jun 1976
1 54.9	T Kazankina	USSR	Montreal	26 Jul 1976
1 54.9	N Olizarenko	USSR	Moscow	12 Jun 1980
1 53.5	N Olizarenko	USSR	Moscow	27 Jul 1980
1 53.28	J Kratochvilova	Czech	Munich	26 Jul 1983

1,500 metres

min sec

4 17.3	A Smith	GB	Chiswick	3 Jun 1967
4 15.6	M Gommers	Netherlands	Sittard	24 Oct 1967
4 12.4	P Pigni	Italy	Milan	2 Jul 1969
4 10.7	J Jehličková	Czech	Athens	20 Sep 1969
4 09.6	K Burneleit	E Germany	Helsinki	15 Aug 1971
4 06.9	L Bragina	USSR	Moscow	18 Jul 1972
4 06.5	L Bragina	USSR	Munich	4 Sep 1972
4 05.1	L Bragina	USSR	Munich	7 Sep 1972
4 01.4	L Bragina	USSR	Munich	9 Sep 1972
3 56.0	T Kazankina	USSR	Podolsk	28 Jun 1976
3 55.0	T Kazankina	USSR	Moscow	6 Jul 1980
3 52.5	T Kazankina	USSR	Zurich	13 Aug 1980

Mile

min sec

4 37.0	A Smith	GB	Chiswick	3 Jun 1967
4 36.8	M Gommers	Netherlands	Leicester	14 Jun 1969
4 35.3	E Tittel	W Germany	Sittard	20 Aug 1971
4 29.5	P Pigni-Cacchi	Italy	Viareggio	8 Aug 1973
4 23.8	N Marasescu	Rumania	Bucharest	21 May 1977
4 21.7	N Marasescu	Rumania	Auckland	27 Jan 1979
4 22.7	M Decker	US	Auckland	26 Jan 1980
4 20.89	L Veselkova	USSR	Bologna	12 Sep 1981
4 18.08	M Decker-Tabb	US	Paris	9 Jul 1982
4 17.44	M Puica	Rumania	Rieti	16 Sep 1982

3,000 metres

min sec

8 52.8	L Bragina	USSR	Durham	6 Jul 1974
8 46.6	G Andersen	Norway	Oslo	24 Jun 1975
8 45.4	G Andersen-Waitz	Norway	Oslo	21 Jun 1976
8 27.2	L Bragina	USSR	College Park	7 Aug 1976
8 26.78	S Ulmasova	USSR	Kiev	25 Jul 1982

100 metres hurdles

sec

13.3	K Balzer	E Germany	Warsaw	20 Jun 1969
13.3	T Sukniewicz	Poland	Warsaw	20 Jun 1969

13.0	K Balzer	E Germany	Leipzig	27 Jul 1969
12.9	K Balzer	E Germany	Berlin	5 Sep 1969
12.8	T Sukniewicz	Poland	Warsaw	20 Jun 1970
12.8	C Chi	Taiwan	Munich	12 Jul 1970
12.7	K Balzer	E Germany	Berlin	26 Jul 1970
12.7	T Sukniewicz	Poland	Warsaw	20 Sep 1970
12.7	K Balzer	E Germany	Berlin	25 Jul 1971
12.6	K Balzer	E Germany	Berlin	31 Jul 1971
12.5	A Ehrhardt	E Germany	Potsdam	15 Jun 1972
12.5	P Kilborn-Ryan	Australia	Warsaw	28 Jun 1972
12.3	A Ehrhardt	E Germany	Dresden	22 Jul 1973

Automatic Timing since 1 May 1977

12.59	A Ehrhardt	E Germany	Munich	8 Sep 1972
12.48	G Rabsztyn	Poland	Fürth	10 Jun 1978
12.36	G Rabsztyn	Poland	Warsaw	12 Jun 1980

400 metres hurdles

sec

56.5	K Kacperczyk	Poland	Augsburg	13 Jul 1974
55.74	T Storozheva	USSR	Karl-Marx-Stadt	26 Jun 1977
55.63	K Rossley	E Germany	Helsinki	13 Aug 1977
55.44	K Kacperczyk	Poland	Berlin	18 Aug 1978
55.31	T Zelentsova	USSR	Podolsk	19 Aug 1978
54.89	T Zelentsova	USSR	Prague	2 Sep 1978
54.78	M Makeyeva	USSR	Moscow	27 Jul 1979
54.28	K Rossley	E Germany	Jena	17 May 1980
54.02	A Ambrosene-Kastetskaia	USSR	Moscow	11 Jun 1983

4 × 100 metres relay

sec

46.6	Germany	Berlin	8 Aug 1936
46.1	Australia	Helsinki	27 Jul 1952
45.9	United States	Helsinki	27 Jul 1952
45.9	Germany	Helsinki	27 Jul 1952
45.6	USSR	Budapest	20 Sep 1953
45.6	USSR	Mocow	11 Sep 1955
45.2	USSR	Kiev	27 Jul 1956
45.1	Germany	Dresden	30 Sep 1956
44.9	Australia	Melbourne	1 Dec 1956
44.9	Germany	Melbourne	1 Dec 1956
44.5	Australia	Melbourne	1 Dec 1956
44.4	United States	Rome	7 Sep 1960
44.3	United States	Moscow	15 Jul 1961
43.9	United States	Tokyo	21 Oct 1964
43.9	USSR	Leninakan	16 Aug 1968
43.6	USSR	Mexico	27 Sep 1968
43.4	United States	Mexico	19 Oct 1968

43.4	Netherlands		Mexico	19 Oct 1968
42.8	United States		Mexico	20 Oct 1968
42.8	W Germany		Munich	10 Sep 1972
42.6	E Germany		Potsdam	1 Sep 1973
42.6	E Germany		Berlin	24 Aug 1974
42.5	E Germany		Rome	8 Sep 1974

Automatic Timing since 1 May 1977

42.51	E Germany		Rome	8 Sep 1974
42.50	E Germany		Karl-Marx-Stadt	29 May 1976
42.27	E Germany		Potsdam	19 Aug 1978
42.10	E Germany		Karl-Marx-Stadt	10 Jun 1979
42.09	E Germany		Turin	4 Aug 1979
42.09	E Germany		Berlin	9 Jul 1980
41.85	E Germany		Potsdam	13 Jul 1980
41.60	E Germany		Moscow	1 Aug 1980
41.53	E Germany		E Berlin	31 Jul 1983

4×400 metres relay

min sec

3 47.4	Moscow (USSR)		Moscow	30 May 1969
3 43.2	Latvia (USSR)		Minsk	1 Jun 1969
3 37.6	Great Britain		London	22 Jun 1969
3 34.2	France		Colombes	6 Jul 1969
3 33.9	W Germany		Athens	19 Sep 1969
3 30.8	Great Britain		Athens	20 Sep 1969
3 30.8	France		Athens	20 Sep 1969
3 29.3	E Germany		Helsinki	15 Aug 1971
3 28.8	E Germany		Colombes	5 Jul 1972
3 28.5	E Germany		Munich	9 Sep 1972
3 23.0	E Germany		Munich	10 Sep 1972
3 19.2	E Germany		Montreal	31 Jul 1976
3 19.04	E Germany		Athens	11 Sep 1982

High jump

metres

1.65	J Shiley	US	Los Angeles	7 Aug 1932
1.65	M Didrikson	US	Los Angeles	7 Aug 1932
1.66	D Odam	GB	Brentwood	29 May 1939
1.66	E Van Heerden	S Africa	Stellenbosch	29 Mar 1941
1.66	I Pfenning	Switzerland	Lugano	27 Jul 1941
1.71	F Blankers-Koen	Netherlands	Amsterdam	30 May 1943
1.72	S Lerwill	GB	London	7 Jul 1951
1.73	A Chudina	USSR	Kiev	22 May 1954
1.74	T Hopkins	GB	Belfast	5 May 1956
1.75	I Balas	Rumania	Bucharest	14 Jul 1956
1.76	M McDaniel	US	Melbourne	1 Dec 1956

1.76	I Balas	Rumania	Bucharest	13 Oct 1957
1.77	C Feng-Yung	China	Beijing	17 Nov 1957
1.78	I Balas	Rumania	Bucharest	7 Jun 1958
1.80	I Balas	Rumania	Cluj	22 Jun 1958
1.81	I Balas	Rumania	Poiana Stalin	31 Jul 1958
1.82	I Balas	Rumania	Bucharest	4 Oct 1958
1.83	I Balas	Rumania	Bucharest	10 Oct 1958
1.84	I Balas	Rumania	Bucharest	21 Sep 1959
1.85	I Balas	Rumania	Bucharest	6 Jun 1960
1.86	I Balas	Rumania	Bucharest	9 Jul 1960
1.87	I Balas	Rumania	Bucharest	15 Apr 1961
1.88	I Balas	Rumania	Warsaw	18 Jun 1961
1.90	I Balas	Rumania	Budapest	8 Jul 1961
1.91	I Balas	Rumania	Sofia	16 Jul 1961
1.92	I Gusenbauer	Austria	Vienna	4 Sep 1971
1.92	U Meyfarth	W Germany	Munich	4 Sep 1972
1.94	Y Blagoyeva	Bulgaria	Zagreb	24 Sep 1972
1.94	R Witschas	E Germany	Berlin	24 Aug 1974
1.95	R Witschas	E Germany	Rome	8 Sep 1974
1.96	R Witschas-Ackermann	E Germany	Dresden	8 May 1976
1.96	R Witschas-Ackermann	E Germany	Dresden	3 Jul 1977
1.97	R Witschas-Ackermann	E Germany	Helsinki	14 Aug 1977
1.97	R Witschas-Ackermann	E Germany	Berlin	26 Aug 1977
2.00	R Witschas-Ackermann	E Germany	Berlin	26 Aug 1977
2.01	S Simeoni	Italy	Brescia	4 Aug 1978
2.01	S Simeoni	Italy	Prague	31 Aug 1978
2.02	U Meyfarth	W Germany	Athens	8 Sep 1982
2.03	U Meyfarth	W Germany	Crystal Palace	21 Aug 1983
2.03	T Bykova	USSR	Crystal Palace	21 Aug 1983
2.04	T Bykova	USSR	Pisa	25 Aug 1983

Long jump

metres

5.98	K Hitomi	Japan	Osaka	20 May 1928
6.12	C Schulz	Germany	Berlin	30 Jul 1939
6.25	F Blankers-Koen	Netherlands	Leiden	19 Sep 1943
6.28	Y Williams	NZ	Gisborne	20 Feb 1954
6.28	G Vinogradova	USSR	Moscow	11 Sep 1955
6.31	G Vinogradova	USSR	Tbilisi	18 Nov 1955
6.35	E Krzesinska	Poland	Budapest	20 Aug 1956
6.35	E Krzesinska	Poland	Melbourne	27 Nov 1956
6.40	H Claus	W Germany	Erfurt	7 Aug 1960
6.42	H Claus	W Germany	Berlin	23 Jun 1961
6.48	T Shchelkanova	USSR	Moscow	16 Jul 1961

6.53	T Shchelkanova	USSR	Leipzig	10 Jun 1962
6.70	T Shchelkanova	USSR	Moscow	4 Jul 1964
6.76	M Rand	GB	Tokyo	14 Oct 1964
6.82	V Viscopoleanu	Rumania	Mexico	14 Oct 1968
6.84	H Rosendahl	E Germany	Turin	3 Sep 1970
6.92	A Voigt	W Germany	Dresden	9 May 1976
6.99	S Siegl	W Germany	Dresden	19 May 1976
7.07	V Bardauskiené	USSR	Kishinyov	18 Aug 1978
7.09	V Bardauskiené	USSR	Prague	29 Aug 1978
7.15	A Cusmir	Rumania	Bucharest	1 Aug 1982
7.20	V Ionescu	Rumania	Bucharest	1 Aug 1982
7.21	A Cusmir	Rumania	Bucharest	14 May 1983
7.43	A Cusmir	Rumania	Bucharest	4 Jun 1983

Shot

metres

14.38	G Mauermayer	Germany	Warsaw	15 Jul 1934
14.59	T Sevryukova	USSR	Moscow	4 Aug 1948
14.86	K Tochonova	USSR	Tbilisi	30 Oct 1949
15.02	A Andreyeva	USSR	Ploesti	9 Nov 1950
15.28	G Zibina	USSR	Helsinki	26 Jul 1952
15.37	G Zibina	USSR	Frunze	20 Sep 1952
15.42	G Zibina	USSR	Frunze	1 Oct 1952
16.20	G Zibina	USSR	Malmö	9 Oct 1953
16.28	G Zibina	USSR	Kiev	14 Sep 1954
16.29	G Zibina	USSR	Leningrad	5 Sep 1955
16.67	G Zibina	USSR	Tbilisi	15 Nov 1955
16.76	G Zibina	USSR	Tashkent	13 Oct 1956
17.25	T Press	USSR	Nalchik	26 Apr 1959
17.42	T Press	USSR	Moscow	16 Jul 1960
17.78	T Press	USSR	Moscow	13 Aug 1960
18.55	T Press	USSR	Leipzig	10 Jun 1962
18.55	T Press	USSR	Belgrade	12 Sep 1962
18.59	T Press	USSR	Kassel	19 Sep 1965
18.67	N Chizhova	USSR	Sochi	28 Apr 1968
18.87	M Gummel	E Germany	Frankfurt	22 Sep 1968
19.07	M Gummel	E Germany	Mexico	20 Oct 1968
19.61	M Gummel	E Germany	Mexico	20 Oct 1968
19.72	N Chizhova	USSR	Moscow	30 May 1969
20.09	N Chizhova	USSR	Chorzów	13 Jul 1969
20.10	M Gummel	E Germany	Berlin	11 Sep 1969
20.10	N Chizhova	USSR	Athens	16 Sep 1969
20.43	N Chizhova	USSR	Athens	16 Sep 1969
20.43	N Chizhova	USSR	Moscow	29 Aug 1971
20.63	N Chizhova	USSR	Sochi	19 May 1972
21.03	N Chizhova	USSR	Munich	7 Sep 1972
21.20	N Chizhova	USSR	Lvov	28 Aug 1973
21.60	M Adam	E Germany	Berlin	6 Aug 1975
21.67	M Adam	E Germany	Karl-Marx-Stadt	30 May 1976

21.87	I Khristova	Bulgaria	Belmeken	3 Jul 1976
21.89	I Khristova	Bulgaria	Belmeken	4 Jul 1976
21.99	H Fibingerova	Czech	Opava	26 Sep 1976
22.32	H Fibingerova	Czech	Nitra	20 Aug 1977
22.36	I Slupianek	E Germany	Celje	2 May 1980
22.45	I Slupianek	E Germany	Potsdam	11 May 1980

Discus
metres

48.31	G Mauermayer	Germany	Dresden	11 Jul 1936
53.25	N Dumbadze	USSR	Moscow	8 Aug 1948
53.37	N Dumbadze	USSR	Gori	27 May 1951
53.61	N Romashkova	USSR	Odessa	9 Aug 1952
57.04	N Dumbadze	USSR	Tbilisi	18 Oct 1952
57.15	T Press	USSR	Rome	12 Sep 1960
57.43	T Press	USSR	Moscow	15 Jul 1961
58.06	T Press	USSR	Sofia	1 Sep 1961
58.98	T Press	USSR	London	20 Sep 1961
59.29	T Press	USSR	Moscow	18 May 1963
59.70	T Press	USSR	Moscow	11 Aug 1965
61.26	L Westermann	W Germany	São Paulo	5 Nov 1967
61.64	C Spielberg	E Germany	Regis Breitingen	26 May 1968
62.54	L Westermann	W Germany	Werdohl	24 Jul 1968
62.70	L Westermann	W Germany	Berlin	18 Jun 1969
63.96	L Westermann	W Germany	Hamburg	27 Sep 1969
64.22	F Melnik	USSR	Helsinki	12 Aug 1971
64.88	F Melnik	USSR	Munich	4 Sep 1971
65.42	F Melnik	USSR	Moscow	31 May 1972
65.48	F Melnik	USSR	Augsburg	24 Jun 1972
66.76	F Melnik	USSR	Moscow	4 Aug 1972
67.32	A Menis	Rumania	Constanta	23 Sep 1972
67.44	F Melnik	USSR	Riga	25 May 1973
67.58	F Melnik	USSR	Moscow	10 Jul 1973
69.48	F Melnik	USSR	Edinburgh	7 Sep 1973
69.90	F Melnik	USSR	Prague	27 May 1974
70.20	F Melnik	USSR	Zürich	20 Aug 1975
70.50	F Melnik	USSR	Sochi	24 Apr 1976
70.72	E Jahl	W Germany	Dresden	12 Aug 1978
71.50	E Jahl	W Germany	Potsdam	10 May 1980
71.80	M Vergova	Bulgaria	Sofia	13 Jul 1980
73.26	G Savinkova	USSR	Lessilidze	22 May 1983

Javelin
metres

46.74	N Gindele	US	Chicago	18 Jun 1932
47.24	A Steinheuer	Germany	Frankfurt	21 Jun 1942
48.21	H Bauma	Austria	Vienna	29 Jun 1947
48.63	H Bauma	Austria	Vienna	12 Sep 1948
49.59	N Smirnitskaya	USSR	Moscow	25 Jul 1949
53.41	N Smirnitskaya	USSR	Moscow	5 Aug 1949

53.56	N Konyayeva	USSR	Leningrad	5 Feb 1954
55.11	N Konyayeva	USSR	Kiev	22 May 1954
55.48	N Konyayeva	USSR	Kiev	6 Aug 1954
55.73	D Zatopková	Czech	Prague	1 Jun 1958
57.40	A Pazera	Australia	Cardiff	24 Jul 1958
57.49	B Zalogaitite	USSR	Tbilisi	30 Oct 1958
57.92	E Ozolina	USSR	Leselidze	3 May 1960
59.55	E Ozolina	USSR	Bucharest	4 Jun 1960
59.78	E Ozolina	USSR	Moscow	3 Jul 1963
62.40	Y Gorchakova	USSR	Tokyo	16 Oct 1964
62.70	E Gryziecka	Poland	Bucharest	11 Jun 1972
65.06	R Fuchs	E Germany	Potsdam	11 Jun 1972
66.10	R Fuchs	E Germany	Edinburgh	7 Sep 1973
67.22	R Fuchs	E Germany	Rome	3 Sep 1974
69.12	R Fuchs	E Germany	Berlin	10 Jul 1976
69.32	K Schmidt	US	Fürth	11 Sep 1977
69.52	R Fuchs	E Germany	Dresden	13 Jun 1979
69.96	R Fuchs	E Germany	Split	29 Apr 1980
70.08	T Biryulina	USSR	Moscow	12 Jul 1980
71.88	A Todorova	Bulgaria	Zagreb	15 Aug 1981
72.40	T Lillak	Finland	Helsinki	29 Jul 1982
74.20	S Sakorafa	Greece	Khania	26 Sep 1982
74.76	T Lillak	Finland	Tampere	13 Jun 1983

Heptathlon

points	100 m hurdles	shot	high jump	200 metres	long jump	javelin	800 metres
6716	R Neubert E Germany			Kiev		27/28 Jun 1981	
	13.70	15.41	1.86	23.58	6.82	40.62	2 06.72
6772	R Neubert E Germany			Halle		19/20 Jun 1982	
	13.59	15.10	1.83	23.14	6.84	42.54	2 06.16
6836	R Neubert E Germany			Moscow		18/19 Jun 1983	
	13.42	15.25	1.82	23.49	6.79	49.94	2 07.51

Steve Ovett and Seb Coe (GB) battle for the 1,500 metres gold medal in Moscow.

THE FIRST WORLD CHAMPIONSHIPS

Athletics finally joined the ranks of the independent when the International Amateur Athletic Federation (IAAF) staged its first World Championships, in Helsinki in 1983. And what a refreshing occasion it was. Even though 157 countries took part — the largest global representation of any event in sports history — the championships went off without boycotts or political intervention of any kind. How long these championships will be free from such confrontation is a matter for speculation. But at the moment, it seems that such troubles are confined chiefly to the Olympic Games. The Olympics needs athletics much more than athletics needs the Olympics, and the World Championships were planned to run alongside rather than replace them.

It is not before time that the athletics bodies got together to produce such an occasion. The opening in Finland proved the fulfilment of a lifetime ambition for some, and was, without doubt, the biggest step ever taken by the IAAF. The rewards were plentiful — so many nations coming together, bringing 1,572 athletes and over 800 officials, all of whom the IAAF paid, to produce seven days of outstanding competition. Over 400,000 paid in excess of £2 million to witness the occasion first-hand, while another billion a day watched on television, emphasizing the growing interest in a sport that was in the doldrums little more than a decade ago. Another bright spot was the IAAF's declaration that over 200 drug tests were taken and not one proved positive. The statement, however, was met with scepticism in many quarters, and proved, perhaps, that while the tests have become more sophisticated, certain athletes have become just that little bit more cunning.

The Americans and the West Germans, who had boycotted the 1980 Olympics in Moscow, took their places alongside the Russians and the Africans, who turned out in force. The Americans proved they had been sadly missed in Moscow, as they swept to victory in the 100 and 200 metres as well as in the 110 and 400 metres hurdles. Outstanding were the performances of one of the sport's millionaires, Carl Lewis, who proved a giant in the 100 metres and the long jump, with comprehensive victories, and then anchored the American sprint relay squad to the gold and a world record. And of their women, Mary Decker became the darling of the track with her two thrilling victories in the 1,500 and 3,000 metres.

Britain's Steve Cram became the brightest star of men's middle-distance running when he won the 1,500 metres. He took some of the limelight from Britain's other gold-medallist, Daley Thompson, perhaps because we have become so used to the latter's successes — Olympic, European, Commonwealth, and now World Champion — a unique collection of gold medals.

But the World Championships were a truly international

affair, and no one will be able to forget the performances of Jarmila Kratochvilova, the powerfully built Czechoslovakian who astounded everyone — except herself — by completing the almost impossible double of the 400 and 800 metres golds, with a world record in the shorter distance, when at one time she had just 30 minutes to spare between competing in the semi-final of one and running the final of the other. Nor would anyone have denied Greta Waitz her victory in the marathon, for this truly outstanding Norwegian has been one of the greatest ambassadors the sport has ever seen. And the sight of the enormous Helena Fibingerova overpowering everyone around and showering kisses upon officials who dare not object, after she won the discus competition, was another joy to behold — at least for those at a safe distance.

Ed Moses, who had been deprived of the chance to defend his Olympic title in Moscow, glided to victory in the one-lap hurdles. And Calvin Smith, who only days previously had broken Jim Hines' 15-year-old world 100 metres record, gained consolation for his defeat in the short sprint by winning the 200 metres. Eamonn Coghlan did Ireland proud with his 5,000 metres gold medal, as did Robert De Castella for Australia in winning the marathon.

But the championships had their hard-luck stories too. Henry Marsh, the American champion, was one such athlete for

Eamonn Coghlan (Eire) wins the 5,000 metres.

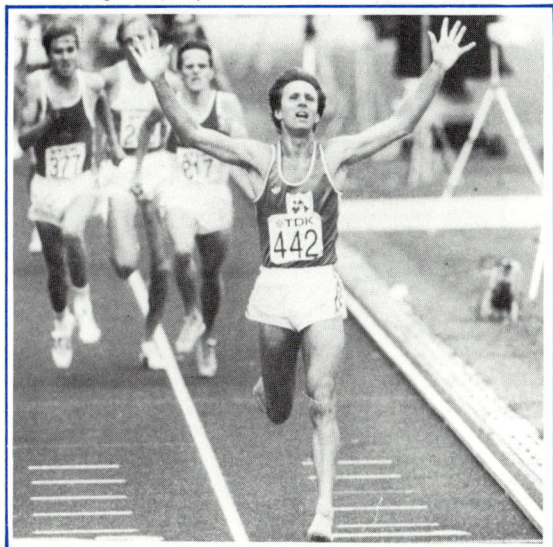

whom all hearts opened as he went into the final obstacle in the 3,000 metres steeplechase with the bronze medal assured, only to tumble over and leave the way open for Britain's Colin Reitz. Alberto Juantorena, the splendid Cuban who had made such a magnificent comeback after injuries almost ruined his career following his Olympic successes in the seventies, collided with a trackside kerb after his heat of the 800 metres, and was ruled out of the rest of the championships with a leg injury. The prospect of the greatest women's 100 metres final in history was also ruined by the suspect thighs of the great American Evelyn Ashford, who broke down after 40 metres against Marlies Gohr and Marita Koch, and hobbled off as the East Germans went on to the gold and silver.

The field events, too, had their ups and downs, especially for Britain's triple jump favourite Keith Connor, who failed to get past the qualifiers. The American Willie Banks could manage only the silver, leaving the unexpected Zdzislaw Hoffman of Poland to succeed. For the British, disappointment came in the javelin, where Fatima Whitbread, for so long in the shadow of Tessa Sanderson, set the competition alight with a first-round throw of 69.14 metres, which put her into the gold-medal position until the final round. But then Tiina Lillak, the darling of the Finns, produced her glorious effort of 70.82 metres to snatch the championship, an effort that had the crowd almost delirious and the blond-haired Miss Lillak doing a sprint around the track. But Fatima had no need to be disappointed, for she was the last of the qualifiers and not many had expected her to win a medal let alone the silver.

Also among the casualties was Olympic high jump champion Sara Simeoni of Italy, the former world record holder, who crashed heavily during the competition and had to be carried off. The episode stunned the Italian people and silenced the Italian Press Corps, who were the most vociferous of press men cramped into the media positions.

It is difficult to level criticism at such a splendid gathering, and in the words of Dr Primo Nebiolo, the IAAF president, 'It was an occasion with honesty, respect, and friendship'. Rome in 1987 will have something to live up to. However, the IAAF must search deeply into the qualifying standards, for, while several countries had to leave good performers behind, many others had qualified athletes who did not deserve to be in the same stadium.

It is also the concensus of opinion that the games could be staged every two years instead of the proposed four, fitting nicely into a pattern with the Olympics, European, and Commonwealth Championships, now that the World and European Cups are on the decline. For many of those who won gold medals, Helsinki was their moment of glory, while for those who failed, the Los Angeles Olympics became even more important.

GREAT ATHLETES

IOLANDA BALAS

(born 12 December 1936)

A Romanian high jumper, Balas dominated her event as no other field events athlete has done, male or female. Using the outmoded scissors style, she set 14 world records. Between 1958 and 1961, she added 14cm to the high jump mark, and it was another 10 years before this was beaten. She also won two Olympic titles (1960 and 1964) and two European titles (1958 and 1962).

ROGER BANNISTER

(born 23 March 1929)

Now Sir Roger, born at Harrow, he was the Coe-Cram-Ovett rolled into one of the mid-fifties. It was at Iffley Road, Oxford, on 6 May 1954, that he produced the first sub four minute mile —an achievement that will always be remembered. It received worldwide acclaim at the time and Bannister's name became synonymous with the mile.

With the invaluable help of Chris Chataway and Chris Brasher, the originators of the pacemaking so frequently used today, Bannister recorded 3 min 59.4 sec to lower Gunder Haegg's nine-year-old record by almost two seconds.

Bannister's record stood for less than two months with John Landy moving faster, but the Australian could not steal the glory. Bannister did gain some revenge by beating Landy in the Commonwealth Games, in what was described then as the duel of the decade, to record a personal best 3 min 58.8 sec.

He later won the European 1500 metres title, but he never won the Olympic gold medal. The closest he got was in 1952 in Helsinki, when, never the strongest of athletes, he had to endure three hard races in as many days. He finished fourth in the UK record time of 3 min 46.0 sec.

Bannister's career was short but exciting. He moved into medicine and was knighted in 1975.

BOB BEAMON

(born 29 August 1946)

Born in New York, Beamon's claim to fame was an incredible leap of 8.90 metres during the 1968 Olympics in Mexico— 29ft 2½ in—when the rest of the world were struggling to clear 27ft. It is a record that has only come under threat with the appearance of Carl Lewis.

It was a leap that astonished everyone, including Britain's

Lynn Davies who had won the gold medal four years earlier in Tokyo. It made nonsense of the previous 30 years, in which the gap had been increased by the merest of decimals.

It also became a one-off, for never again did Beamon get near his achievement; according to the record books, he never got past 8.20 metres after Mexico. In fairness, he did suffer serious hamstring injuries to his right leg, and finally turned professional in 1973.

ABEBE BIKILA

(1932-1973)

As a virtual unknown and running barefoot, Ethiopian soldier Abebe Bikila won the 1960 Olympic marathon in 2hr 15min 16.2sec, a world's best time. In 1964 he became the first man to win the Olympic marathon twice, recording another world's best with 2hr 12min 11.2sec, finishing fresh and a record 4min 8sec in front of the next man. And this was only 6 weeks after having his appendix out. In 1968 a serious leg injury forced his retirement from the Olympics. A year later he received severe injuries in a car crash, which left him paralysed and led to his death in 1973.

FANNY BLANKERS-KOEN

(born 26 April 1918)

Born in Amsterdam, Francina Koen was destined to become the best known post-war athlete in the world with her amazing performance of collecting four gold medals at the Olympic Games in London in 1948, coached by her husband, Jan Blankers.

She won the 100 and 200 metres and 80 m hurdles and was the anchor leg of the sprint relay squad that took the gold. Among her other medal performances were eight medals, including five golds, from three European Championships.

In a career that really began in the mid-1930s and was interrupted by the war years, she managed to hold world records at seven different events, and as late as 1956—at 38 years old—she could still run 11.3 sec for the hurdles.

RALPH BOSTON

(born 9 May 1939)

Born in Laurel, Mississippi, Boston was the man who broke Jesse Owens' long jump record, becoming the first man to leap over 27 ft.

He won the Olympic title in 1960 in Rome and four years later finished runner up to Lynn Davies in Tokyo, then third to Bob Beamon four years later in Mexico.

But both before and after these successes, he was outstanding, increasing the world record to 8.28 metres and then regaining it after losing it to Ter-Ovanesyan of Russia, with 8.35 metres.

RON CLARKE

(born 21 February 1937)

Clarke, born in Melbourne, currently lives in London where he is in charge of a sports complex in the City of London. He was without doubt, the 'wonder boy' of Australian athletics, making an enormous impact on the record books, but never winning a major title.

He set records for the 2 miles, 3 miles, 5,000 metres, 6 miles, 10,000 metres, 10 miles, 20,000 metres and the one hour. He was largely responsible for the increase in popularity of middle distance running.

He was favourite to win the 10,000 metres title in the Tokyo Olympics but finished third and stood little chance in the altitude of Mexico four years later.

Altogether, he won three silver medals at the Commonwealth Games from 1962 to 1966 and finally bowed out with yet another silver at the Commonwealth Games in the 10,000 metres in 1970.

He was also a prolific setter of world junior records. He saw his first Olympics in Melbourne in 1956 not as an athlete but as the carrier of the torch at the opening ceremony.

SEBASTIAN COE

(born 29 September 1956)

Coe, from Chiswick in London, came out from behind the shadow of Steve Ovett with a devastation of world records in 1979 when he set new times for the mile, 1500 and 800 metres all within the space of 41 days.

Yet his superiority at 800 metres running has failed him in the Olympics and European Championships. He was struck down with glandular trouble in Athens in 1982, recurring midway through 1983, to destroy his hopes in the World Championships. But the rare illness, diagnosed as glandular toxoplasmosis, is just another hurdle that Coe believes he will overcome.

Coe, in fact, set out to be a sprinter in his schooldays, but had switched to cross country and 1500 metres running by the time he was 16. He won his first major title, the European

Indoor 800 metres, in San Sebastian. He lost only one race the following year but it was the most important, the European Championship in Prague, where he finished third to Jurgen Straub and Ovett—his first encounter on the track with his great rival.

The accent on speed took over in 1979, and, coached by his father Peter, he erased the name of Juantorena with a world 800 metres record of 1 min 42.33 sec on 5 July in Oslo. He returned there 12 days later to win the golden mile in 3 min 48.95 sec, another world record. Then after victories in Viareggio and Turin in the European Cup, he chose Zurich for his third record and broke the 1500 metres time with 3 min 32.03 sec.

He was installed as Olympic 800 metres favourite and he went to Bislett just before Moscow to break the world 1,000 metres time with 2 min 13.40 sec. The Olympics proved a disaster at 800 metres, with a tactical error relegating him to second place behind Ovett, but two days later he reversed the positions in the 1500 metres.

The following year started superbly with an indoor 800 metres record at Cosford and then an outdoor time of 1 min 41.73 sec in Florence. Despite atrocious pacemaking he recorded a personal best 1500 metres in Stockholm. He improved his 1,000 metres time in Oslo and finished off the season by breaking the mile record twice in nine days, first in Zurich with 3 min 48.53 sec and when Ovett broke it a week later, he reclaimed it in Brussels with 3 min 47.33 sec.

But disaster struck in Athens in 1982 when, leading off the final bend in the European Championships 800 metres, his power deserted him and he was beaten by Hans Peter Ferner. He appeared to be on the mend at the start of 1983 when he set the world 800 metres indoor record at Cosford and then added the indoor 1,000 metres to his credit in Oslo. But when he lost track races in Paris, London and Gateshead, despite a fast 800 metres in between, he quit for the season.

STEVE CRAM

(born 14 October 1960)

Cram, from Gateshead, is the young pretender who became king when Britain's time as masters of middle distance was running out, due to the injuries and illness of Coe and Ovett.

Winner of the 1982 European 1500 metres title in Athens and the Commonwealth Championship a month later in Brisbane, he completed the hat-trick by becoming World Champion in Helsinki in 1983, beating Ovett. However, it was his race at Crystal Palace several weeks later than confirmed him as the world's best at the distance, when he outran Ovett once more.

Cram was not exactly new to championship running before these successes, for he had appeared in the Commonwealth

Games as far back as 1978 at 17 years old, an age at which he held the group world record. In 1980, not yet 20, he finished eighth in the Olympic 1500 metres final.

Suffering leg injuries, Cram did not have much time to train for his Helsinki triumph but he came through with 3 mins 35.77 sec, holding off Steve Scott's final straight challenge. A week later he was at Crystal Palace winning the European Cup final for Britain in 3 min 42.27 sec. After a period chasing world records, unsuccessfully, in Europe, he came back to Crystal Palace and before a full house, won that classic race with Ovett.

BETTY CUTHBERT

(born 20 April 1938)

An Australian sprinter, Betty Cuthbert broke 11 individual world records from 60 metres to 440 yards and enjoyed a double career. Born at Merrylands, near Sydney, she was, at 18, unprepared for the success she achieved at the Melbourne Olympics in 1956, when she performed the sprint double and won a third gold medal in the relay. Eight years later, she made a remarkable comeback in Tokyo to win the 400 metres Olympic title.

LYNN DAVIES

(born 20 May 1942)

A Welshman born in Nantymoel, Davies became that country's first Olympic Champion by winning the long jump in Tokyo in 1964. He was inevitably named 'Lynn the Leap'. Davies' victory had been entirely unexpected for no Briton had won a field event at the Games for almost 60 years and the field included Ralph Boston and Igor Ter-Ovanesyan. However, his fifth round effort of 8.07 metres, off a saturated cinder runway, was good enough to push him into gold medal position.

It was also the start of the Golden quest for Davies for he went on to capture the Commonwealth title with 7.99 metres and in addition the European title with 7.98 metres in 1966. He retained his Commonwealth title in 1970.

ROBERT DE CASTELLA

(born 27 February 1957)

De Castella's convincing marathon victory in the 1983 World Championships confirmed him as the world No.1. With a world best 'out-and-back' time of 2hr 8min 18sec to his credit at Fukuoka in 1981, De Castella looks a good bet to win back the marathon record Alberto Salazar (USA) took from his fellow Australian Derek Clayton two months earlier with a time only 5 seconds better in the New York event.

SHIRLEY DE LA HUNTY

(born 18 July 1925)

Mrs De la Hunty, born Strickland in Guildford, Western Australia, collected a total of seven Olympic medals, and it might have been eight.

It was in the London Olympics of 1948 that Miss Strickland appeared to have finished third in the 200 metres, only to be given fourth place. Yet 28 years later when the photo finish film was published for the first time, it showed her in the bronze position.

She was third in the 80 metres hurdles in the 1948 Games but became Champion in 1952 and retained the title in Melbourne. She was also bronze medallist in the 100 metres in 1948 and 1952 and collected a silver for the sprint relay in 1948. Eight years later, she earned another gold in the same squad. In addition, she won two gold and two silver medals at the Commonwealth Games.

MILDRED DIDRIKSON

(1914-1956)

One of the most remarkable female athletes of all time, 'Babe' Didrikson won the American women's team championships in 1932 single-handed. Born at Port Arthur Texas, the 'Babe' excelled at every sport she took up. Restricted to three events at the 1932 Olympics, she won golds in the hurdles and javelin and was relegated to second place in the high jump by a dubious judging decision. She took up golf, and as Mrs Zaharias she became the best woman golfer in the world, winning tournament after tournament in the 1940s and early 1950s. She died of cancer in 1956, but not before she had come back after an operation to win her third US Open in 1954.

HARRISON DILLARD

(born 8 July 1923)

Born in Cleveland, USA, Dillard's name became a byword in Britain in 1948 with his outstanding success at the London Olympics.

Inspired to become an athlete with the sight of Jesse Owens

being paraded through the streets of his hometown after the 1936 Olympics, Dillard achieved his first world record in the 220 yards in 1946.

Between May 1947 and June 1948, he won 82 successive sprint and hurdle races, yet he fell in the US Olympic trials that year and failed to make the hurdles squad.

But his third place qualified him for Wembley at 100 metres and he equalled Owens' Olympic record of 10.3 sec and four years later won the hurdles title in Helsinki.

HERB ELLIOTT

(born 25 February 1938)

Born in Subiaco, Perth, Elliott from the age of 16 until he retired in 1962, never lost a mile or 1500 metres out of a total of 45 races, winning the Olympic title in 1960 in Rome and the Commonwealth Games gold medals at the 1958 Games at both the 880 yards and the mile.

Classed as the greatest miler of all time, Elliott was running 4 min 25.6 sec at 16, and was a sensation at Cardiff in 1958 when he finished off an eight-day spell of record breaking that included the mile at 3 min 54.5 sec and the 1500 metres at 3 min 36.0 sec, by winning the 880 yards gold in a record 1 min 47.3 sec.

Such was the aura surrounding Elliott, just as it is with Ovett, Cram and Coe today, that he was reported to have rejected an offer of almost £90,000 to turn professional.

DICK FOSBURY

(born 6 March 1947)

Born in Portland, Oregon, Fosbury revolutionised the high jump with his famous 'flop' style of jumping that won him the 1968 Olympic title and has now become the accepted style for the event.

He began the experiments, that were to win him the gold, as a 16 year-old and by the time he had left school he was clearing two metres and recorded 7ft as a 20 year-old.

In 1968 he cleared 2.24 metres to win the title, a height that is still only one centimetre below the current British record, but he was lost to the sport five years later when he turned professional.

WALTER GEORGE

(1858-1943)

Born at Calne, Wiltshire, George, or WG as he was known, was one of the first superstars of the track with a collection of world records from the mile, in 4 min 18.4 sec, through to the

10 miles, as well as a bevy of English titles.

His match with William Cummings in 1886 was the equivalent of a Coe-Cram-Ovett encounter nowadays. He won in 4 min 12 sec. He ran the 10 miles in 1886 in 49 min 29 sec, a time that was not beaten for 60 years.

MARLIES GOHR

(born 21 March 1958)

Born in Gera, East Germany, she made up for all the disappointments of not winning the Blue riband of sprinting, the Olympic 100 metres title in Moscow, by taking the World Championships in Helsinki in 1983.

It was a race that became a let-down however for the German who was matched against her great American rival Evelyn Ashford, for the American broke down during the running and Mrs Gohr went on to victory in 10.97 sec, beating her compatriot Marita Koch.

She also collected a gold medal as a member of the 4×100 metres relay at the same Games and to complete a tremedous season, won the European Cup final sprint at Crystal Palace.

Considered the fastest female ever, she finished eighth in the Montreal Olympic final of 1976 at the age of 18, but was a member of the German gold medal winning relay team and when it came to Moscow she was considered the favourite, only to suffer a surprise defeat by Ludmila Kondratyeva. Again she picked up the gold in the relay squad.

She was also second to the Russian in the 1978 European Championships, but gained the gold four years later in Athens.

After being beaten by Mrs Ashford in the 1979 World Cup she had to taste defeat again to the American in 1971 in Rome where she surprisingly finished in third place.

MURRAY HALBERG

(born 7 July 1933)

Born in Eketahuna, North Island, New Zealand, Halberg turned to athletics when a rugby accident in 1950 paralysed his left arm. He became a fine miler, but it was at longer distances that he eventually excelled. Famed for his lung-bursting surges from three laps from home, he won the Olympic 5000 metres title in 1960 in between his two Commonwealth 3 miles titles and he set world records at 2 and 3 miles.

JIM HINES

(born 10 September 1946)

When Hines, who was born in Dumas, Arkansas, ran 9.9 sec at

the AAU Championships in Sacramento in 1968, he staked his claim to a place in the history of the sport, for he was the first man to break the 10 sec barrier with a legal time after earlier running a wind assisted 9.8 sec. He won the Olympic title in Mexico the same year with 9.95 sec.

MARJORIE JACKSON

(born 13 September 1931)

Australian sprinter Marjorie Jackson retired at 22 with an extraordinary collection of world records and major titles to her name. Born in Lithgow, New South Wales, she equalled or set 10 world records, including a phenomenal 10.4 sec 100 yards in 1952 that knocked 3/10ths of a second off her own two-years-old mark, achieved the sprint double at the 1952 Olympics, and won seven individual and relay gold medals at the 1950 and 1954 Commonwealth Games.

BRUCE JENNER

(born 28 October 1949)

Born in New York, Jenner was considered the greatest all rounder until Daley Thompson appeared on the scene. He won the decathlon title at the 1976 Olympics with a world record score adding more than 160 points to the total which had brought Avilov the title in Munich. He was a typical jack-of-all events, master of none, but it was the basis of his success, and his good looks added to his popularity. He is said to be one of the athletes who have moved into millionaire status.

ALBERTO JUANTORENA

(born 21 November 1950)

Born in Santiago, he became the man to beat when he burst upon the scene with his reputed nine-foot stride, to win the 800 metres in Munich with a world record time of 1 min 43.50 sec. He went on to win the 400 metres, his main event at that stage, in 44.26 sec, then ran a leg of the relay, but was denied a medal.

A one-time basketball player, Juantorena switched to running in 1971 defeating David Jenkins in the World Student Games two years later and heading the world rankings in 1974.

A foot injury in 1975 looked as if it had slowed the giant down but he proved the critics wrong by breaking the world 800 metres record and completing a double in the World Cup at 400 and 800 metres.

Once again injuries and illness struck but yet he came back to run in Moscow in 1980 at 400 metres and finished in fourth place. In 1983 the Cuban suffered another of the mishaps that have haunted him all his life when, running in a heat of the 800 metres at the World Championships, he won but then tripped, damaging his ankle severely enough to put him out for the rest of the season.

But the 'big man' is not finished, for he intends to be in Los Angeles and to win the gold medal there.

KIP KEINO

(born January 1940)

Born in Kipsamo, Keino is one of the great Kenyans who have thrilled British fans over the past decades with their fearless front running.

A Kenyan and East Africa Champion at 22, he moved from 11th place in the 1962 Commonwealth Games to 5th in the Olympic final in Tokyo, two years later, at 5,000 metres but it was a year later that he made the world sit up and take notice.

Then he twice beat Ron Clarke over 5,000 metres; set a world record of 7 min 39.6 sec for the 3,000 metres and was a shade outside the world mile time with 3 min 54.2 sec. While in New Zealand he broke the world 5,000 metres with 13 min 24.2 sec.

He carried his success into 1966, winning the Commonwealth Games gold medals at 800 and 1500 metres, the first time the event had been included in the Games.

A regular at meetings throughout the world after that, running anything from 800 to 10,000 metres, Keino collected an Olympic gold at 1500 metres in 1968, the Commonwealth 1500 metres gold two years later and then in Munich won the Olympic steeplechase gold to add to various silver and bronze medals from these events.

MARITA KOCH

(born 18 February 1957)

Marita Koch, from Wismar, East Germany, reached the pinnacle of her career by winning the Olympic 400 metres title in Moscow in 1980 and then three years later made it a double by winning the World Championship gold—but this time at 200 metres.

A most adaptable athlete, Miss Koch has had the misfortune at one lap running to be matched with the great Irena Szewinska during the first part of her career and now with Jarmila Kratochvilova, but she had few rivals over 200 metres.

She made her mark in 1975 when winning the silver medal

at the European Junior Championships only to suffer disappointment a year later in Montreal when injury cost her a place in the final of the Olympics.

In 1977 at the European Indoor Championships, she won the 400 metres in a world record 51.14 sec and then followed that with victory in the European Cup final.

She lost to Szewinska in the World Cup final but made amends in the 1978 European Championship final with a world record of 48.94 sec.

She was beaten by Evelyn Ashford in the 1979 World Cup final but by then had set the world records for both the 200 and 400 metres.

She beat Kratochvilova in the final of the European Cup 400 metres in Athens in 1971 but a few weeks later the powerful Czech reversed the order in the World Cup in Rome.

Apart from the 200 metres gold in Helsinki, the German also collected a silver in the 100 metres, a gold for the sprint relay but had the disappointmet of seeing her world 400 metres record go to Kratochvilova.

JARMILA KRATOCHVILOVA

(born 26 January 1951)

Born in Gorcuv, near Prague, this powerfully built Czech girl became the sensation of the first World Championships in Helsinki in 1983 by winning the semi final of the 400 metres and then, less than 30 minutes later, returning to the track to win the 800 metres gold medal.

It was a time gap that many experts said was impossible to bridge. Then she defied everyone by taking the one lap gold a day later and did it in a world record time.

Her arrival on the world scene was delayed until she was 25 by a series of injuries and illnesses and it was not until 1978 that her name began to appear regularly. Even then she was eliminated at the semi final stage of the European Championships in Prague, where Britain's Joslyn Hoyte Smith finished ahead of her in both the heat and the semi final although neither went through.

Six months later in the European Indoor Championships in Vienna she had to be content with the silver medal, this time it was Britain's Verona Elder who got up from behind on the last lap, to win the gold.

The major medals eluded her again in 1980 at the Moscow Olympics when she was well beaten in the 400 metres by Marita Koch but Jarmila, one of a large family, who dedicated her life to athletics and training, was not finished. In 1981 at the age of 30, she gained her revenge over Koch, by beating her in both the European and World Cup finals, although the following year, she was once again demoted to the silver medal in the European Championships by Koch.

Then in 1983 came the momentous double task, with tough races every day. On the Tuesday in Finland she produced an 800 metres time of 1 min 54.68 sec and the following day the first sub 48 sec for a woman, with a record of 47.99 sec.

With times in all races from the 100 to 800 metres faster than the British records, she came to England a week after Helsinki to win the 200 and 800 metres in the European Cup, preferring to leave the 400 metres title to her team mate Kocembova.

VLADIMIR KUTS

(1927-1975)

Born in Aleksinko, USSR, the world lost a great athlete when Kuts died after a heart attack in 1975.

The successor to Zatopek, Kuts' first claim to fame was when he unofficially broke the world 3 mile record during a 5,000 metres race.

But it was in 1954 that he surprised everyone by running away from the field early in the European Championships 5,000 metres and staying out front to win the gold medal, beating Chataway and Zatopek in a world record of 13 min 56.6 sec.

His great enemies were the English. He lost the 5,000 metres and the record to Chataway in London in 1954 and was beaten by Pirie and again lost the record, this time in Norway.

But he gained his revenge over Pirie at the Melbourne Olympics when he won first the 10,000 metres and then the 5,000 metres. Just before the games he added the world 10,000 and 5,000 metres records to his impressive list of honours.

JOHN LANDY

(born 4 April 1930)

Unfortunate to be overshadowed when it mattered by Roger Bannister, Australian miler John Landy set world mile and 1500 metres records in 1954. As a front runner, he fell victim to Bannister's sprint finish in the classic Vancouver encounter that year and to Ron Delany's in the 1956 Olympics. He is remembered, too, for his fine sportsmanship.

CARL LEWIS

(born 1 July 1961)

Born Frederick, Carlton, in Birmingham, Alabama, Lewis had a fortunate start for his parents were not only teachers, but dad was a track coach and his mother a former international hurdler.

He became an overnight sensation in Helsinki when millions of television viewers saw him flit between the long jump and the 100 metres winning the gold medal at both and also a third gold for the 4×100 metres relay where he anchored the squad to a new world record.

Lewis, set to become one of the millionaires of athletics, has brought the day closer when it may be possible that someone will break the long jump record that Bob Beamon set in Mexico in 1968.

Lewis has cleared the 28ft mark on numerous occasions and his 28ft 10in in 1983 in Indianapolis at the US Championships, is the best ever at sea level. Earlier in the same meeting he had recorded 19.75 sec, again the fastest 200 metres at sea level.

He went to Helsinki for the World Championships with all the flare of a superstar, and he proved he was. He outran Calvin Smith, the world 100 metres record holder, in the final with Olympic champion Allan Wells in fourth.

In the long jump he killed off all the opposition with his first effort of 8.55 metres and then produced another of 8.42 metres which would also have won him the gold, just for good measure.

Then with Emmit King, Willie Gault and Calvin Smith, produced 37.86 sec against the world relay record of 38.03 sec. It is likely that he could have won the 200 metres as well; almost certain he will attempt four golds in Los Angeles in order to equal the 1936 record of his childhood hero, Jesse Owens.

Among his other notable victories has been the World Cup long jump title in Rome in 1981.

BRONISLAW MALINOWSKI

(1951-1981)

Born in Nowe, Poland, a tragic car accident brought to an end the career of possibly the greatest steeplechaser the world is ever likely to see.

A popular figure in Britain, Malinowski who boasted a Scottish mother and said at one time he would like to run for that country, first made his mark when he won the European junior 2,000 metres title in 1970.

He later went on to win the European senior 3,000 metres title in 1974 and 1978 but had to wait for three Olympics before finally winning the gold as he did in Moscow, coming back from over 30 metres behind to win in 8 min 9.7 sec.

In 1972 in Munich he had been fourth and four years later in Montreal he got inside the world record but still had to be content with the silver behind Anders Garderud of Sweden.

He did not restrict his running to steeplechasing, for apart from being a frequent competitor in cross country events, he had a best of 1 min 49.8 sec for the 800 metres and 28 min 25.2 sec for the 10,000 metres.

BOB MATHIAS

(born 17 November 1930)

Born in Tulare, California, Mathias was the subject of a feature film in which he played himself. In later life he became a US congressman—but it was on the track that he first became famous.

At the age of 17, Mathias astounded London by winning the decathlon gold medal at Wembley, a title which he successfully defended four years later setting three world records during that time.

Mathias had suffered from anaemia as a youngster, but such was his fighting spirit that he became champion of California in the discus by the time he was 16 and with such a prowess for all events, made his decathlon debut a year later.

Although he was declared a professional in 1953, he continued to compete in the services and his record of being unbeaten from 1948 to 1956 stands.

DAVID MOORCROFT

(born 10 April 1954)

From Coventry in England, Moorcroft's finest performance was undoubtedly breaking the world 5,000 metres record in Oslo in 1982 when he took off so early and won by so much that Ralph King, of the US, the next man home thought that he had won the race! 'I was under the impression that when the man in front took off, he was just another pacemaker and had dropped out later on and I could not understand why the clock had stopped at 13 min 0.42 sec when I crossed the line,' said King. But it was true, Moorcroft had not just lowered the record set by Henry Rono a year earlier in Bergen, but had shattered it by a massive 5.78 sec.

Recently, Moorcroft has been dogged by injury and illness in his preparation for the Los Angeles Olympics.

EDWIN MOSES

(born 31 August 1955)

Born in Dayton, Ohio, Moses is poetry in motion as far as 400 metres hurdling is concerned. He has won 87 consecutive finals (at the time of writing) and promised that when it reaches 100, he will turn to 800 metres running.

Unbeaten since he lost to Harald Schmidt in August 1977, Moses is in fact well over the 90 mark in victories but refuses to count heats and in Koblenz in 1983 he rounded off a fantastic series of races in Europe by setting a new world record of 47.02 sec, needless to say it was his own record he broke.

An outspoken critic of drugs in sport, Moses has also made a name for himself in broadcasting which he did in 1982 when he took the complete season off to recuperate from injuries.

His biggest blow was not being able to defend his Olympic title in Moscow because of the boycott by the United States but only a major disaster will prevent him recapturing it in Los Angeles.

Moses rarely runs less than 49 sec, a time that most would be proud to achieve and of the world's top 10 times at 400 metres hurdling, he holds nine.

Moses burst upon the scene in 1976 after a rather obscure start of ordinary 110 metre hurdling and flat 400 metres running. He began the Montreal Olympic year, however, at 50.1 sec after his coach had realised his ability at 400 metres hurdling and then proceeded to chop almost seconds off that time on every occasion that he ran. He was in peak form for the Olympics shattering the world record in the final with 47.64 sec.

He made up for the disappointment of missing Moscow by winning the World Championship in Helsinki in 1983 and there is little doubt that when he finally retires, the world will not produce another hurdler like him.

RENALDO NEHEMIAH

(born 24 March 1959)

Born in Newark, New Jersey, athletics lost another in the Moses mould when he decided to switch from 110 metres hurdling to the world of American football, at which he is now a great success.

Renaldo or 'skeets' as he is known, ran the heart out of the European hurdlers in 1980 but because of the American ban was not allowed to chase what he wanted most, the Olympic title in Moscow.

There can be little doubt that he would have been the odds on favourite for the title, won by Thomas Munkelt. He is still the world record holder for the event, with the 12.93 sec set in Zurich in 1981.

Nehemiah made his mark at high school, breaking record after record and it was in 1979 that he eliminated the name of Alejandro Casanas of Cuba from the record books when he recorded 13.16 sec, only to run even faster, 13 sec flat, when he won the Pan American games and the World Cup.

He is a useful long jumper as well as a flat 100 and 200 metres runner.

PAAVO NURMI

(1897-1973)

Born in Turku, Nurmi is regarded as the greatest athlete Finland ever produced and his statue stands proudly at the entrance of the Olympic stadium in Helsinki.

Nurmi deserves all the adulation of the Finns, winning every honour in his sport in a career that stretched over 20 years, ending when he won the National 1500 metres title in 1933 at the age of 36.

But before that he had amassed nine Olympic medals beginning with a gold in the 10,000 metres and a silver for the 5,000 metres in 1920 followed by the 1500, 5,000 metres, the cross country and the 3,000 metres team race four years later.

In 1928 in Amsterdam, he won the 10,000 metres and took the silver in the 5,000 and 3,000 metres steeplechases. He was all set to contest the 1932 marathon only to be disqualified for professionalism.

He also achieved remarkable successes in the indoor season and an abundance of world records, including one for the 10 miles that lasted over 16 years.

Paavo Nurmi wins the 5,000 metres in the 1924 Olympics.

AL OERTER

(born 19 September 1936)

Born in Astoria, New York, Oerter is a living legend among discus throwers, winning the Olympic gold medal four times, the last being in 1968. He can still be seen competing at meetings around Europe despite being in his late forties.

After Mexico, Oerter decided to give the 1972 Olympics a miss and faded into the background but he came back in 1977, ready to make the 1980 team that eventually boycotted Moscow.

He won his first Olympic gold in Melbourne in 1956 but he had to wait six years for his first world record and at the same time became the first man to throw over 200 feet (61.10 metres). He lost and reclaimed it several times after that although he was always the competitor first and record breaker second. Even in 1980 he could still throw 69.46 metres which at that time, ranked him second in the world.

STEVE OVETT

(born 9 October 1955)

From Brighton, England, Ovett's illustrious career almost came to an abrupt end during an early evening training run near his south-coast home in December 1981, when he ran into church railings, puncturing the muscles above his right knee. With all the determination that had gained him so many honours and victories, Ovett came back to run the world record in Rieti in September 1983, a month after coming fourth in the World Championships in Helsinki.

Ovett's career began in 1970 when he won his first title, the English schools Junior 400 metres, in 51.8 sec. He got a taste for record breaking in 1971, setting the UK 14 year age group record for the 800 metres in 1 min 55.3 sec.

What fans at Crystal Palace in 1975 did not realise when John Walker beat Ovett in the mile was that it was to be his last defeat at that distance for another six years—a sequence ended by Sydney Maree in Rieti in 1981—four days after Ovett had won the World Cup 1500 metres in Rome.

But in between that time Ovett established himself as a competitive athlete who wanted to run first and break records afterwards, in 1977 winning the European Cup final and the World Cup final, the latter in 3 min 34.5 sec, a UK record.

In 1978, he was second in the European Championships 800 metres, winning his first ever encounter with Seb Coe who took the bronze. He made no mistake, winning the 1500 metres title at the same meeting.

Ovett had to wait until July 1980 before setting his first official world record. Spurred on by the success of Coe, Ovett used Bislett to produce a 3 min 48.8 sec mile and then 15 days later equalled the 1500 metres record with 3 min 32.1 sec.

It was the Moscow Olympics, however, that produced the surprises. In two unforgettable races he outpaced Coe for the 800 metres title—and then finished third behind him in the 1500 metres, to end a sequence of 45 races at a mile or 1500 metres without defeat.

He returned to break the world 1500 metres record in Koblenz with 3 min 31.36 sec, set the world one mile record a year later and then won the World Cup 1500 metres in Rome. 1982 was planned as the year of a three-series clash with Coe, in London, Nice and Eugene only for that to be ruled out through injuries.

While Coe struggled through 1983, Ovett ran a poor World Championships 1500 metres final but came back to break the world record once again just a week after Maree had taken it from him.

JESSE OWENS

(1913-1980)

Born in Daneville, Alabama, he was the greatest pre-war athlete, considered a physical genius by many who saw him perform.

He is best known for the 'Hitler' Olympics in Berlin of 1936 where he won four gold medals, including winning the long jump in which he had almost failed to qualify, with a leap of 8.06 metres.

Yet the statisticians consider that Owens had done even better a year earlier at Ann Arbor, Michigan, when he equalled the 100 yards world record, set a long jump world record of 8.13 metres that lasted 25 years, set another world record for the 220 yards straight in 20.3 sec and then ran the 220 yards hurdles in another world record.

He began his career at an early age with some of his school figures still the envy of modern day athletes, including a 7.61 metres long jump. After his success in Berlin, Owens turned professional and in 1948 he was still long jumping at around 7.90 metres. In 1955 at the age of 41, he ran the 100 metres in 9.8 sec. It was a tribute that both Harrison Dillard and later Carl Lewis based their early training on him.

MARY RAND

(born 10 February 1940)

Born in Wells, Somerset, Mary now lives in the US with her second husband Bill Toomey, the Olympic decathlon champion, whom she married in 1969.

The golden girl of British athletics in the sixties, Mary Bignall as she then was, made her presence felt as a 17-year-old when she set the pentathlon record. A year later she gained the long jump silver at the Commonwealth Games.

Her first Olympics, Rome in 1970, were a disaster for she had led the overnight qualifiers in the long jump, to eventually finish ninth. However, she did manage to finish fourth in the hurdles.

She was married to Sid Rand the Olympic sculler, and despite the birth of her daughter in 1962, she was fit enough to win the European long jump bronze.

She achieved her Olympic gold in the long jump with a world record 6.76 metres, a distance that was to stand until the

World Championships in Helsinki as a British best, when Bev Kinch put together a series of six leaps all over it.

HENRY RONO

(born 12 February 1952)

Born in Kaprirsang in Kenya, Henry, or Kipwambok as he was named, a member of the Kalenjin tribe, amazed the athletics world in 1978 when he set the world records for the 3,000 metres, 5,000 and 10,000 metres as well as the 3,000 metres steeplechase all within three months.

Three of those still stand today, only the 5,000 metres has gone, broken by David Moorcroft in Oslo in 1982.

He had set the 5,000 metres at Berkeley in April, then in May went to Seattle to break the steeplechase time of Anders Garderud and moved into Europe in the June to break the 10,000 metres time of his countryman Samson Kimobwa in Vienna. Then in Oslo's famous Bislett Stadium, he finished off his escapades by relieving Brendan Foster of his world 3,000 metres record with 7 min 32.1 sec.

Running anything from the steeplechase to 10,000 metres and the half marathon, Rono was a Commonwealth Champion but was deprived of his Olympic ambitions when the Africans boycotted first the Montreal games and then the Moscow games four years later.

WILMA RUDOLPH

(born 23 June 1940)

A classic case of triumph over adversity, Wilma Rudolph was the crippled child of a poor black family who went on to win Olympic glory. Born in Tennessee, one of 19 children, she lost the use of a leg through illness at four and did not walk again till she was seven. Yet she grew up to be a tall, elegant sportswoman and at 16 won a bronze relay medal at the 1956 Olympics. Four years later in Rome, she won both sprints and a third gold medal in the relay. She also set world records in the 100 and 200 metres.

JIM RYUN

(born 29 April 1947)

Born in Wichita, Kansas, Ryun was another of the famous record breakers who found that the major championship gold medals eluded him. He cut short his brilliant amateur career by turning professional in 1972.

Considered one of the greatest milers of all time, he held age group bests that Steve Cram later broke but it was as a

19-year-old that he first found fame, running 3 min 51.3 sec to smash the record held by Peter Snell.

He was also record holder for the 880 yards with 1 min 44.9 sec and for the 1500 metres with 3 min 33.1 sec but his attempts to win Olympic golds always ended in disaster.

In 1964, he was the youngest member of the US team in Tokyo and failed to reach the final of the 1500 metres after suffering from heavy colds. Four years later in Mexico, he could not beat the high altitude or Kip Keino and then in Munich he tripped over during the running of the 1500 metres and was eliminated.

VIKTOR SANEYEV

(born 3 October 1945)

Russian triple jumper Saneyev was a supreme competitor, winning three Olympic golds and narrowly failing to equal Oerter's unique four-timer at Moscow in 1980 when at 34 he was beaten by fellow-countryman Jaak Uudmae. His first success, in 1968, came in that memorable competition in which the world record was surpassed five times, twice by Saneyev himself, who went on to notch his third world record with 17.44 metres in 1972.

ALF SHRUBB

(1897-1964)

Born in Slinfold, Sussex, Shrubb can be considered the father of British middle distance champions, holding every record from the 1½ miles to the one hour.

He began running in 1898 and three years later won the first of his national titles, the AAA championship at the mile. He claimed the 1903 and 1904 international cross country championships and was considered a certainty for a medal in the 1904 Olympics in St Louis, but Britain decided against sending a team.

He was declared a professional, later, and included among his paid tricks a 10 miles race against a horse. He coached the Oxford University squad before he moved to Canada in 1928. He was reinstated by the AAA as an amateur in 1953.

PETER SNELL

(born 17 December 1938)

Born in Opunake, New Zealand, Snell was to dominate middle distance running in the early sixties, as he chased the records of Herb Elliott.

He will be best remembered as the man who did the double of golds for the 800 and 1500 metres at the Tokyo Olympics but it was in 1962 that he first began his assault on major honours and records by clipping a tenth of a second of Elliott's world one mile record with 3 min 54.5 sec. He set new times for the 800 metres, 1 min 44.3 sec, and 1 min 45.1 sec for the 880 yards.

He had won the Olympic title in 1960 at 800 metres, the Commonwealth 880 yards of 1962, as well as the mile but a year after his Tokyo successes decided to retire from the sport.

He did not confine his running to 800 and 1500 metres, actually recording 2 hr 41 min 11 sec for a marathon.

IRENA SZEWINSKA

(born 24 May 1946)

Born in Leningrad, but always a member of the Polish squad, Mrs Szewinska enjoyed the title of European queen of athletics for many years. Beginning as an 18-year-old at the Tokyo Olympics, she won the silver medal for the long jump; gained another in the 200 metres in a European record time and then helped Poland win the 4×400 metres in a world record.

She set world records for both sprints in 1965 and then won the 200 metres and the long jump at the European Championships a year later, as well as helping Poland win the sprint relay.

In 1968 in Mexico, she won the Olympic 200 metres gold with a world record of 22.58 sec and also picked up a bronze in the 100 metres.

More bronze medals followed in the European Games and the Olympics of 1972 before she started serious 400 metres running in 1973, setting world records leading up to the breaking of the 50 sec barrier.

She emphasised her tremendous ability by winning the 400 metres in the Montreal Olympics of 1976 in a world record 49.28 sec. She even competed in the Moscow Olympics—her fifth—but at 34 her career came to an end with a leg injury and she was eliminated in the semi final stage.

One of the most popular athletes of all time, Mrs Szewinska is a constant visitor to England.

DALEY THOMPSON

(born 30 July 1958)

Born in London of a Nigerian father and a Scottish mother, Thompson is without question the greatest all-round athlete the world has ever seen with his decathlon victories at two Commonwealth Games, European Championships, Olympics and World Championships. He considers himself young enough to win them all the way to Seoul in 1988.

Francis Morgan Thompson, to give him his real name, dreamed of becoming a soccer player, began sprinting, then moved into the decathlon to win the Welsh Open with 6,685 points in 1975—at just 17 years of age. A year later he reached the Montreal Olympics finishing 18th with 7,435 points. In 1977 he set a world junior record at Gotzis in Austria where twice in later years he was to set the senior record.

In 1978 he won the Commonwealth Games title in Edmonton with a score of 8,467, but it was in Olympic year that he really surpassed himself, first breaking Bruce Jenner's world record in Gotzis with 8,622 points, only to lose it shortly afterwards to West German Guido Kratschmer.

He tried desperately to recapture it at the Moscow Olympics later in the year and with an overnight score of 4,542 appeared certain to do so but a change in the conditions on the second day made him settle for the gold.

In 1982 Thompson completed the clean sweep, starting when he regained the world record again in Gotzis in May with 8,704 points. Jurgen Hingsen, another West German went even better shortly afterwards, but Thompson put them all in place by recapturing the world record yet again with 8,743 points and with it the European gold medal. A month later he retained his Commonwealth gold medal in Brisbane.

In 1983, Thompson achieved the clean sweep by winning the World Championships in Helsinki and although Hingsen had taken the world record from him earlier in the year, Thompson had the consolation of finishing 105 points ahead of the German with 8,666 points.

JIM THORPE

(1888-1953)

Born in Oklahoma part American-part Indian, Thorpe died in 1953 long before he could learn that he was to be reinstated as an amateur and his medals returned.

The subject of the film 'Man of Bronze' played by Burt Lancaster, Thorpe was the Daley Thompson of the early 1900s, his career culminating in the winning of the Olympic pentathlon and decathlon titles at the 1912 Olympic Games.

They were victories that were to turn sour, for in January the following year, it was disclosed that he had in fact played baseball for which he had been paid, and he was stripped of everything including his dignity.

After his imposed professionalism, Thorpe went on to play not only baseball but football and he received the consolation of being voted the greatest footballer in America.

WYOMIA TYUS

(born 29 August 1945)

Born at Griffin, Georgia, Wyomia made the sprinting Europeans sit up and take notice in 1964 when she set an indoor world record of 7.5 sec for the 70 yards, but it was at the 1964 Olympics in Tokyo that she really stamped her name in the hall of fame by first equalling the world 100 metres record in the heats and then winning the final.

In 1965 she equalled the world records for the 100 metres and 100 yards. She achieved a first when she defended her 100 metres title at the Mexico Olympics and also managed to set the world record of 11.08 sec.

LASSE VIREN

(born 22 July 1949)

Born in Myrskyla, Viren became the hero of Finland when he followed in the traditions of Finnish greats by completing the double of 5,000 and 10,000 metres gold medals at the Munich Olympics, the latter at which he set a world record of 27 min 38.4 sec, despite falling during the race!

Four years later, despite looking an also-ran in the in between years, he went to Montreal and retained both his titles and then ran into 5th place in the marathon only 24 hours after winning the 5,000 metres gold.

After another four years of mediocre performances dotted by injuries and illness, Viren attempted to do the impossible at Moscow and when he took the lead in the 10,000 metres with 1200 metres to go, he appeared to have achieved it, only to be beaten on the final lap and eventually finish in fifth place.

His first notice on the athletic scene had been posted when he set a world two miles record shortly before Munich and then added a 5,000 metres best later that year.

His only other medal of note, however, came in the 1974 European Championships when he gained the bronze in the 5,000 metres.

GRETA WAITZ

(born 1 October 1953)

Born in Oslo, Mrs Waitz is the greatest woman long distance runner of all time. When she won the World Championships marathon in Helsinki in 1983, there was never a more popular and fitting winner. Slimly built and blond, she first came to the forefront in 1974 by winning the bronze medal at 1500 metres at the European Championships, as Greta Andersen. It was 12 months later that she decided to increase her distance and shattered the world 3,000 metres record with 8 min 46.6 sec, then lowered it by almost a second in 1976, the year of the Olympics.

With a longer distance than 1500 metres for women still a way off, Mrs Waitz failed to make the final—and lost her world record shortly afterwards to Lyudmila Bragina. Although she never got near that time, the Norwegian did have the consolation of beating Bragina in the World Cup final a year later. In 1978, she moved into marathon running. In New York she lowered the existing world record by over two minutes with a time of 2 hr 32 min 30 sec.

She has dominated cross country—at which she has won five out of the six world titles—and in 1979 set world records for the 10,000 metres, the 10 miles and again the marathon in New York. In 1980, she set a new world record for the 15 kilometres, the 10,000 metres, the indoor 3,000 metres and astonishingly, the marathon record in New York for the third successive time.

JOHN WALKER

(born 12 January 1952)

Born in Papukura, Walker has been a great ambassador for New Zealand running during a period when his country has declined as a world force.

Walker's greatest achievement was winning the 1976 Olympic 1500 metres title in Montreal but it was as a world record breaker that he achieved his fame, especially on the European circuit. Only injury prevented him from increasing his list of achievements. Yet he came back to run his fastest times in 1982 although he had to be content to run as an also-ran in the era of Coe and Ovett.

In 1974 Walker first came to notice in a race that he lost. The occasion was the 1974 Commonwealth Games in Christchurch when Filbert Bayi smashed the 1500 metres world record of Jim Ryun, a time that Walker also got inside in second place, a defeat he made up for in Helsinki later in the year.

He came to Europe a year later and was the first man in racing history to break 3 min 50 sec for the mile, he ran 3 min 49.4 sec.

He broke the 2,000 metres world record of Michel Jazy shortly before the 1976 Olympics with 4 min 51.4 sec, a time that stands today, despite the attempts of Wessinghage, Coe and Ovett.

Dogged by injuries and operations after that, Walker got back to form in readiness to defend his title in 1980 but with the New Zealanders joining in the boycott, despite a protest from the athletes, he had to watch his great rival Coe take the gold.

A great competitor, Walker not often outspoken, upset officialdom in 1983 by warning them of the increasing dangers of drugs that he claimed were in widespread use at the World Championships in Helsinki, where he reached the final of the 1500 metres.

CORNELIUS WARMERDAM

(born 22 June 1915)

For world supremacy in one event, Warmerdam's pole vault record takes some beating. Born in California, the son of Dutch immigrants, Warmerdam was a decade ahead of his time. Using a bamboo pole, he set a world record, his third, in 1942 of 4.77 metres (15ft 7¾in), which stood for 15 years. He retired from amateur competition in 1944 with 43 15-foot vaults to his credit, and it was seven years before another vaulter reached that height.

ALLAN WELLS

(born 3 May 1952)

Wells, from Edinburgh, is without doubt the finest sprinter that Britain has produced, winning the Olympic title in 1980 at 100 metres when four years earlier Britain had not even bothered to send a sprinter to Montreal. Wells' win was the first by a British runner since Harold Abrahams in the famous 'Chariots of Fire' finals in Paris in 1924. In addition, Wells took the silver medal in the 200 metres, beaten this time by his great rival Pietro Mennea of Italy.

In 1978, Wells had won the Commonwealth Games gold for the 200 metres and the relay as well as a silver in the 100 metres.

It was thought that the IAAF ruling that all sprinters must use blocks, which Wells had scorned, would affect him, but he adapted magnificently to achieve success in Moscow where the absence of the US team took some glory off his achievement. He won the Commonwealth Games 100m again in 1982, but then had to settle for a deadheat in the 200 metres with Mike McFarlane.

MIRUTS YIFTER

(born about 1943)

Nicknamed 'Yifter the Shifter' by an English newspaper, Yifter is one of the great mysteries of athletics—not on the track for he is a master—but because of his age for even he has doubts about just how old he is!

In fact, he has had more birth years than Coe or Ovett have broken world records but it is estimated that this great, little, balding man is approaching at least 40!

An officer in the Ethiopian Air Force and father of six children, Yifter sprang to prominence as early as 1970 when he outran Mamo Wolde, the Olympic marathon champion, over 10,000 metres and then beat Kip Keino in a 5,000 metres race.

But Yifter possessed the same inability to count—as he and his countrymen were to display in the World Cross Country 10 years later—when he appeared to have won the 5,000 metres in a match with the Americans in 1971 but sprinted to the line a lap too early. He made no mistake 24 hours later, beating Frank Shorter in the 10,000 metres.

He missed the start of the 5,000 metres in the Munich Olympics and finished third in the 10,000 metres behind Viren but his hopes of succeeding four years later in Montreal were foiled by the African boycott of the games.

He completed the double at the World Cups of 1977 and 1979 and showed Steve Ovett a clean pair of heels when he dashed off the final bend of a rare Ovett 5,000 metres at Gateshead. A year later he joined the immortals by achieving the gold in both the 10,000 and 5,000 metres.

He was a bystander at the 1983 World Championships in Helsinki for he did not make the team, but was in training then for the marathon at the Los Angeles Olympics.

EMIL ZATOPEK

(born 12 September 1922)

Born in Koprivnice—the same day as his wife Dana (nee Ingrova) who was the Olympic javelin champion in 1952, Zatopek brought off the nigh impossible, the gold medals at 5,000 metres, 10,000 metres and the marathon at the Helsinki Olympics to establish himself as a worldwide name.

Yet surprisingly Zatopek who had won the marathon by 1½ laps had never run a competitive race at the distance before then!

It was four years before that the incredible Czech won his first gold, at 10,000 metres at the Wembley Olympics, again less than 10 weeks after running that event for the first time. Not to be outdone he also took the silver in the 5,000 metres.

He won the European Championships titles at both the 5,000 and 10,000 metres in 1950 and the gold for the longer distance four years later.

He set world records in almost monotonous fashion during that time from 5,000 to 30,000 metres and was the first man to break 29 min for the 10,000 metres.

His last Olympic appearance came in the 1956 games in Melbourne when in only the second marathon of his career, he finished in sixth place—yet shortly before that he had undergone a hernia operation.

FINANCIAL REWARDS

When is an amateur athlete not an amateur? This has become a common question in sport. For while some sports, such as cricket, tennis, and football, have reached a compromise, it is baffling to many that athletes can be paid vast sums, either to participate or through advertising, and still remain within the realms of amateur status.

It is only since the IAAF brought some commonsense into the rules of the sport in 1983, with the advent of 'permit' meetings, that athletes have been able to gain some reward for their ability to pack stadiums with spectators. Even so, they have to wait until the end of their careers to claim the majority of benefit. There is no doubt that some have struck it rich. Sebastian Coe and Daley Thompson are cashing in on the television screen by way of advertisements, and Steve Ovett and Steve Cram have been sponsored by rival copier companies. Providing all goes right for them, they should be set for a comfortable life when they retire from athletics.

This method of deferred payment has hopefully eradicated the hypocrisy of the 'shamateur'. It has been said that if the Inland Revenue had made its books public, many famous names would have disappeared from the athletics scene overnight. Apart from inflated expenses, the cash inducement figures reported in foreign newspapers following meetings, although denied by the promoters, must give rise to some speculation. Officials seem to have been aware of what was going on, but generally could not prove it. Only when payments have been most blatant has action been taken, but, even then, in several cases the athlete concerned has been reinstated after suffering a short term of suspension. Top athletes from several countries have disclosed that they received 'under the counter' payments for appearances — but only after they had retired from the sport.

Many query why the Western athletes should be so strictly rule-bound when their Eastern European counterparts have the benefit of being 'employed' as forces personnel as a cover for their activities as full-time athletes. Western athletes often have to give up their jobs to concentrate on athletics, and it appears that almost all are seeking sponsorships, whether from the Sports Aid Foundation, Britain's biggest sponsor, or from suppliers of the small grant scheme, from local companies, up to the major concerns such as Peugeot Talbot, Ubix, and ICI. But one thing can be certain, and that is it is only the few who will make their fortune. The main 'perk' available to the rest is in the supply of cheap or free kit, such as tracksuits and shoes. The majority of the major manufacturers are very keen to provide these items, with the possibility of advertising exposure on television.

The guidelines on how to receive payment and still protect 'amateur' status are now laid down by many individual national bodies, such as the British Amateur Athletic Board. As the BAAB points out, there are still vague areas, but expenses can include claims for assistance in the purchase of sports equipment and clothing, insurance to cover illness, the cost of medical attention, the services of a coach, accommodation, transport, eduction, and professional training.

The situation is best explained by the BAAB's advice guide. Monies made available to athletes are normally provided in one of three ways: by sponsors as subventions; for advertising services; or as participation money.

SUBVENTIONS

This is a gift to an athlete with no advertising strings attached. An example of a subvention is a grant provided for an athlete, for a training trip perhaps, by the Sports Aid Foundation.

All subvention monies have to be paid directly to the BAAB, and are controlled by them. Subvention monies under £500 can be paid to, and controlled by, the athlete's National Athletic Association, should they so desire. Monies received as subventions by the BAAB do not have commission deducted by the BAAB, and the money is placed in a deposit account accruing normal rates of interest, with that interest being used to meet all out-of-pocket administration expenses incurred by the BAAB.

MONEY FROM ADVERTISING

An athlete who is approached with a view to advertising products must ensure that any contract or exchange of letters is with the BAAB, and all monies accruing under that agreement are paid directly to the BAAB. Likewise, if the payment is in kind, the BAAB must also have full details of such arrangements. The BAAB then (a) pay any commission agreed with any agent and (b) extract their own commission. The residue of the contract monies is paid into, and forms, the Athlete's Fund.

If the advertising money totals less than £5,000, the money must not go to the athlete, but directly to the BAAB. On learning of the provisional agreement entered into between the athlete and the advertiser, the BAAB obtain a signed letter of the agreement from the advertiser setting out the responsibilities of the advertiser and athlete. A copy of the letter of agreement is sent to the athlete, requesting the athlete to sign a 'side letter' saying that he has seen the agreement and agrees to abide by his responsibilities as outlined therein.

All monies must be passed to the representative of the BAAB, and placed in the Athlete's Fund on behalf of the athlete. The BAAB levy a flat 10 per cent administrative fee. The Athlete's Fund money is placed in a deposit account, and interest from it is paid into the Athlete's Fund. If payment in kind is involved, then the advertiser must quantify the 10 per cent cost of that provision and pass that amount to the BAAB for administration expenses.

If the advertising money or the money in the fund is, or becomes more than, £5,000, the advertiser must, from the outset, deal only with the General Secretary of the BAAB. When the details of the agreement are made known to the General Secretary, he draws up a formal contract with the advertiser, after seeking appropriate advice. Accompanying the contract will be a detailed form of the trust deed, which will outline just how the Athlete's Fund will be managed. The trust document names the three trustees established under the trust, with two representing the BAAB and one representing the athlete. These three will be responsible for the management of the Trust Fund. The athlete cannot be a direct party to either of the legal documents already drawn up, but will sign a 'side letter' to the effect that he has seen the contract and the trust deed, and agrees to abide by his responsibilities outlined.

An Athlete's Fund will then be established at a major bank, and any claim for payment from the Athlete's Fund will be released by that bank only with the agreement of the trustees, in the case of a full trust document having been executed, or following the agreement of the BAAB General Secretary in other cases. The commission taken by the BAAB will be 15 per cent on the first £50,000, 10 per cent on the next £5,000, and 7½ per cent thereafter on the cumulative total of contracts exceeding £5,000.

PARTICIPATION MONEY

Monies should be negotiated between an athlete and a permit meeting organizer prior to the meeting, and must be forwarded directly to the BAAB immediately after the meeting. Depending on whether it is over or under £5,000, the procedures outlined for the advertising funds apply. The major difference is that the BAAB does not deduct an administration commission percentage from any participation monies.

The BAAB must receive and administer all participation funds on behalf of the athlete. Otherwise, the amateur status of the athlete will be at risk.

INCOME TAX AND ATHLETES' FUNDS

All monies entering an athlete's fund from advertising or participation sources are assessable upon the athlete, subject to allowable expenses permitted by the Inland Revenue. In simple terms, this means for most athletes that whatever monies they accumulate in the Athlete's Fund, taxation will be about 30 per cent after deductions of allowable expenses. It is essential, therefore, that sufficient monies should be left in the fund to deal with the tax on revenues that have come into the fund.

THE BIG MEETINGS

OLYMPIC GAMES

Venues

1896	Athens	1948	London
1900	Paris	1952	Helsinki
1904	St Louis	1956	Melbourne
1908	London	1960	Rome
1912	Stockholm	1964	Tokyo
1920	Antwerp	1968	Mexico
1924	Paris	1972	Munich
1928	Amsterdam	1976	Montreal
1932	Los Angeles	1980	Moscow
1936	Berlin		

MEN

60 metres

			sec
1900	A C Kraenzlein	US	7.0
1904	A Hahn	US	7.0

100 metres

			sec
1896	T Burke	US	12.0
1900	F W Jarvis	US	11.0
1904	A Hahn	US	11.0
1908	R E Walker	South Africa	10.8
1912	R Craig	US	10.8
1920	C Paddock	US	10.8
1924	H M Abrahams	GB	10.6
1928	P Williams	Canada	10.8
1932	T Tolan	US	10.3
1936	J C Owens	US	10.3
1948	H Dillard	US	10.3
1952	L Remingo	US	10.79
1956	B J Morrow	US	10.62
1960	A Hary	Germany	10.32
1964	R Hayes	US	10.05
1968	J R Hines	US	9.95
1972	V Borzov	USSR	10.14
1976	H Crawford	Trinidad	10.06
1980	A Wells	GB	10.25

200 metres

			sec
1900	J W Tewksbury	US	22.2
1904	A Hahn	US	21.6
1908	R Kerr	Canada	22.6
1912	R Craig	US	21.7
1920	A Woodring	US	22.0
1924	J V Scholtz	US	21.6

1928	P Williams	Canada	21.8
1932	T Tolan	US	21.2
1936	J C Owens	US	20.7
1948	M Patton	US	21.1
1952	A Stanfield	US	20.81
1956	B J Morrow	US	20.75
1960	L Berruti	Italy	20.62
1964	H Carr	US	20.38
1968	T C Smith	US	19.83
1972	V Borzov	USSR	20.00
1976	D Quarrie	Jamaica	20.23
1980	P Mennea	Italy	20.19

400 metres

			sec	
1896	T Burke	US	54.2	
1900	M Long	US	49.4	
1904	H Hillman	US	49.2	
1908	W Halswelle	GB	50.0	*
1912	C Reidpath	US	48.2	
1920	B Rudd	South Africa	49.6	
1924	E Liddell	GB	47.6	
1928	R Arbuti	US	47.8	
1932	W Carr	US	46.2	
1936	A Williams	US	46.5	
1948	A Wint	Jamaica	46.2	
1952	V Rhoden	Jamaica	46.09	
1956	C L Jenkins	US	46.86	
1960	O C Davis	US	45.07	
1964	M Larrabee	US	45.15	
1968	L Evans	US	43.86	
1972	V Matthews	US	44.66	
1976	A Juantorena	Cuba	44.26	
1980	V Markin	USSR	44.60	

* Walk over

800 metres

			min sec	
1896	E H Flack	Australia	2	11.0
1900	A E Tyson	GB	2	01.2
1904	J Lightbody	US	1	56.0
1908	M Sheppard	US	1	52.8
1912	J Meredith	US	1	51.9
1920	A G Hill	GB	1	53.4
1924	D G Lowe	GB	1	52.4
1928	D G Lowe	GB	1	51.8
1932	T Hampson	GB	1	49.7
1936	J Woodruff	US	1	52.9
1948	M G Whitfield	US	1	49.2
1952	M G Whitfield	US	1	49.2
1956	T W Courtney	US	1	47.7

1960	P Snell	New Zealand	1	46.3
1964	P Snell	New Zealand	1	45.1
1968	R Doubell	Australia	1	44.3
1972	D Wottle	US	1	45.9
1976	A Juantorena	Cuba	1	43.5
1980	S Ovett	GB	1	45.4

1500 metres

			min	sec
1896	E Flack	Australia	4	33.2
1900	C Bennett	GB	4	06.2
1904	J Lightbody	US	4	05.4
1908	M Sheppard	US	4	03.4
1912	A N Jackson	GB	3	56.8
1920	A G Hill	GB	4	01.8
1924	P J Nurmi	Finland	3	53.6
1928	H E Larva	Finland	3	53.2
1932	L Beccali	Italy	3	51.2
1936	J E Lovelock	New Zealand	3	47.8
1948	H Eriksson	Sweden	3	49.8
1952	J Barthel	Luxembourg	3	45.1
1956	R Delany	Ireland	3	41.2
1960	H J Elliott	Australia	3	35.6
1964	P Snell	New Zealand	3	38.1
1968	K Keino	Kenya	3	34.9
1972	P Vasala	Finland	3	36.3
1976	J Walker	New Zealand	3	39.2
1980	S Coe	GB	3	38.4

5,000 metres

			min	sec
1912	H Kolehmainen	Finland	14	36.6
1920	J Guillemot	France	14	55.6
1924	P Nurmi	Finland	14	31.2
1928	V Ritola	Finland	14	38.0
1932	L Lehtinen	Finland	14	30.0
1936	G Hockert	Finland	14	22.2
1948	G Reiff	Belgium	14	17.6
1952	E Zatopek	Czech	14	06.6
1956	V Kuts	USSR	13	39.6
1960	M Halberg	New Zealand	13	43.4
1964	R K Schul	US	13	48.8
1968	M Gammoudi	Tunisia	14	05.0
1972	L Viren	Finland	13	26.4
1976	L Viren	Finland	13	24.8
1980	M Yifter	Ethiopia	13	21.0

10,000 metres

			min	sec
1912	H Kolehmainen	Finland	31	20.8
1920	P Nurmi	Finland	31	45.8

1924	V Ritola	Finland		30 23.2
1928	P Nurmi	Finland		30 18.8
1932	J Kusocinski	Poland		30 11.4
1936	I Salminen	Finland		30 15.4
1948	E Zatopek	Czech		29 59.6
1952	E Zatopek	Czech		29 17.0
1956	V Kuts	USSR		28 45.6
1960	P Bolotnikov	USSR		28 32.2
1964	W M Mills	US		28 24.4
1968	N Temu	Kenya		29 27.4
1972	L Viren	Finland		27 38.4
1976	L Viren	Finland		27 40.4
1980	M Yifter	Ethiopia		27 42.7

Marathon			hr	min sec	
1896	S Louis	Greece	2	58 50	*
1900	M Theato	France	2	59 45	*
1904	T J Hicks	US	3	28 53	*
1908	J J Hayes	US	2	55 18.4	**
1912	K McArthur	South Africa	2	36 54.8	*
1920	H Kolehmainen	Finland	2	32 35.8	
1924	A Stenroos	Finland	2	41 22.6	
1928	B El Ouafi	France	2	32 57	
1932	J Zabala	Argentine	2	31 36	
1936	K Son	Japan	2	29 19.2	
1948	D Cabrera	Argentine	2	34 51.6	
1952	E Zatopek	Czech	2	23 03.2	
1956	A Mimoun	France	2	25 00	
1960	Abebe Bikila	Ethiopia	2	15 16.2	
1964	Abebe Bikila	Ethiopia	2	12 11.2	
1968	M Wolde	Ethiopia	2	20 26.4	
1972	F Shorter	US	2	12 19.8	
1976	W Cierpinski	E Germany	2	09 55.0	
1980	W Cierpinski	E Germany	2	11 03.0	

* under distance
** D Pietri (Italy) 1st but disqualified

2,500 metres steeplechase			min sec
1900	G Orton	Canada	7 34.4
1904	J Lightbody	US	7 39.6

3,000 metres steeplechase			min sec	
1920	P Hodge	GB	10 0.4	
1924	V Ritola	Finland	9 33.6	
1928	T Loukola	Finland	9 21.8	
1932	V Iso-Hollo	Finland	10 33.4	*
1936	V Iso-Hollo	Finland	9 03.8	

1948	T Sjostrand	Sweden	9 04.6
1952	H Ashenfelter	US	8 45.4
1956	C Brasher	GB	8 41.2
1960	Z Krzyszkowiak	Poland	8 34.3
1964	G Roelants	Belgium	8 30.8
1968	A Biwott	Kenya	8 51.0
1972	K Keino	Kenya	8 23.6
1976	A Garderud	Sweden	8 08.0
1980	B Malinowski	Poland	8 09.7

* almost 500 metres over distance

| **3,200 metres steeplechase** | | | **min sec** |
| 1908 | A Russell | GB | 10 47.8 |

| **4,000 metres steeplechase** | | | **min sec** |
| 1900 | J Rimmer | GB | 12 58.4 |

110 metres hurdles			**sec**
1896	P Curtis	US	17.6
1900	A Kraenzlein	US	15.4
1904	F Schule	US	16.0
1908	F Smithson	US	15.0
1912	F Kelly	US	15.1
1920	E Thomson	Canada	14.8
1924	D Kinsey	US	15.0
1928	S Atkinson	South Africa	14.8
1932	G Saling	US	14.6
1936	F Towns	US	14.2
1948	W Porter	US	13.9
1952	H Dillard	US	13.91
1956	L Calhoun	US	13.70
1960	L Calhoun	US	13.98
1964	W Jones	US	13.6
1968	W Davenport	US	13.33
1972	R Milburn	US	13.24
1976	G Drut	France	13.30
1980	T Munkelt	E Germany	13.39

400 metres hurdles			**sec**
1900	J W Tewksbury	US	57.6
1904	H Hillman	US	53.0
1908	C Bacon	US	55.0
1920	F Loomis	US	54.0
1924	F Taylor	US	52.6
1928	Lord Burghley	GB	53.4
1932	R M Tinsdall	Ireland	51.7
1936	G Hardin	US	52.4
1948	L Cochran	US	51.1

1952	C Moore	US	51.06
1956	G Davis	US	50.29
1960	G Davis	US	49.51
1964	W Cawley	US	49.60
1968	D Hemery	GB	48.12
1972	J Akii-Bua	Uganda	47.82
1976	E Moses	US	47.64
1980	V Beck	E Germany	48.70

4 × 100 metres relay

			sec
1912	Great Britain		42.4
1920	United States		42.2
1924	United States		41.0
1928	United States		41.0
1932	United States		40.0
1936	United States		39.8
1948	United States		40.6
1952	United States		40.26
1956	United States		39.59
1960	Germany		39.66 *
1964	United States		39.0
1968	United States		38.23
1972	United States		38.19
1976	United States		38.33
1980	USSR		38.26

* United States 1st but disqualified

4 × 400 metres relay

		min	sec
1912	United States	3	16.6
1920	Great Britain	3	22.2
1924	United States	3	16.0
1928	United States	3	14.2
1932	United States	3	08.2
1936	Great Britain	3	09.0
1948	United States	3	10.4
1952	Jamaica	3	03.9
1956	United States	3	04.7
1960	United States	3	02.2
1964	United States	3	00.7
1968	United States	2	56.1
1972	Kenya	2	59.8
1976	United States	2	58.7
1980	USSR	3	01.1

High jump

			metres
1896	E H Clark	US	1.81
1900	I K Baxter	US	1.90
1904	S Jones	US	1.80
1908	H Porter	US	1.90
1912	A Richards	US	1.93

1920	R Landon	US	1.93
1924	H Osborn	US	1.98
1928	R King	US	1.94
1932	D McNaughton	Canada	1.97
1936	C Johnson	US	2.03
1948	J Winter	Australia	1.98
1952	W Davis	US	2.04
1956	C Dumas	US	2.12
1960	R Shavlakadze	USSR	2.16
1964	V Brumel	USSR	2.18
1968	R Fosbury	US	2.24
1972	J Tarmak	USSR	2.23
1976	J Wszola	Poland	2.25
1980	G Wessig	E Germany	2.36

Pole vault			metres
1896	W Hoyte	US	3.30
1900	I Baxter	US	3.30
1904	C Dvorak	US	3.50
1908	E Cooke &	US	3.71
	A Gilbert	US	3.71
1912	H Babcock	US	3.95
1920	F Foss	US	4.09
1924	L Barnes	US	3.95
1928	S Carr	US	4.20
1932	W Miller	US	4.31
1936	E Meadows	US	4.35
1948	O G Smith	US	4.30
1952	R Richards	US	4.55
1956	R Richards	US	4.56
1960	D Bragg	US	4.70
1964	F Hansen	US	5.10
1968	R Seagren	US	5.40
1972	W Nordwig	E Germany	5.50
1976	T Slusarski	Poland	5.50
1980	W Kozakiewicz	Poland	5.78

Long jump			metres
1896	E Clark	US	6.35
1900	A Kraenzlein	US	7.18
1904	M Prinstein	US	7.34
1908	F Irons	US	7.48
1912	A Gutterson	US	7.60
1920	W Pettersson	Sweden	7.15
1924	W De Hubbard	US	7.44
1928	E Hamm	US	7.73
1932	E Gordon	US	7.64
1936	J C Owens	US	8.06
1948	W Steele	US	7.82
1952	J Biffle	US	7.57

1956	G Bell	US	7.83
1960	R Boston	US	8.12
1964	L Davies	GB	8.07
1968	R Beamon	US	8.90
1972	R Williams	US	8.24
1976	A Robinson	US	8.35
1980	L Dombrowski	E Germany	8.54

Triple jump

			metres *
1896	J Connolly	US	13.71*
1900	M Prinstein	US	14.47
1904	M Prinstein	US	14.35
1908	T Ahearne	GB	14.91
1912	G Lindblom	Sweden	14.76
1920	V Tuulos	Finland	14.50
1924	A Winter	Australia	15.52
1928	M Oda	Japan	15.21
1932	C Nambu	Japan	15.72
1936	N Tajima	Japan	16.00
1948	A Ahman	Sweden	15.40
1952	A F Da Silva	Brazil	16.22
1956	A F Da Silva	Brazil	16.35
1960	J Szmidt	Poland	16.81
1964	J Szmidt	Poland	16.85
1968	V Sanyeyev	USSR	17.39
1972	V Sanyeyev	USSR	17.35
1976	V Sanyeyev	USSR	17.29
1980	J Uudmae	USSR	17.35

* two hops, one jump

Shot

			metres
1896	R Garrett	US	11.22
1900	R Sheldon	US	14.10
1904	R Rose	US	14.81
1908	R Rose	US	14.21
1912	P McDonald	US	15.34
1920	V Porhola	Finland	14.81
1924	C Houser	US	14.99
1928	J Kuck	US	15.87
1932	L Sexton	US	16.00
1936	H Woellke	Germany	16.20
1948	W Thompson	US	17.12
1952	W P O'Brien	US	17.41
1956	W P O'Brien	US	18.57
1960	W Nieder	US	19.68
1964	D Long	US	20.33
1968	R Matson	US	20.54
1972	W Komar	Poland	21.18
1976	U Beyer	E Germany	21.05
1980	V Kiselyev	USSR	21.35

Discus			metres
1896	R Garrett	US	29.14
1900	R Bauer	Hungary	36.04
1904	M Sheridan	US	39.28
1908	M Sheridan	US	40.88
1912	A Taipale	Finland	45.20
1920	E Niklander	FInland	44.68
1924	C Houser	US	46.14
1928	C Houser	US	47.32
1932	J Anderson	US	49.48
1936	K Carpenter	US	50.48
1948	A Consolini	Italy	52.78
1952	S Iness	US	55.02
1956	A Oerter	US	56.32
1960	A Oerter	US	59.18
1964	A Oerter	US	61.00
1968	A Oerter	US	64.78
1972	L Danek	Czech	64.40
1976	M Wilkins	US	67.50
1980	V Rashchupkin	USSR	66.64

Hammer			metres
1900	J Flanagan	US	49.72
1904	J Flanagan	US	51.22
1908	J Flanagan	US	51.92
1912	M McGrath	US	54.74
1920	P Ryan	US	52.86
1924	F Tootell	US	53.28
1928	P O'Callaghan	Ireland	51.38
1932	P O'Callaghan	Ireland	53.92
1936	K Hein	Germany	56.48
1948	I Nemeth	Hungary	56.06
1952	J Csermak	Hungary	60.34
1956	H Connolly	US	63.18
1960	V Rudenkov	USSR	67.10
1964	R Klim	USSR	69.74
1968	G Zsivoyzky	Hungary	73.36
1972	A Bondarchuk	USSR	75.50
1976	Y Sedykh	USSR	77.52
1980	Y Sedykh	USSR	81.80

Javelin			metres
1908	E Lemming	Sweden	54.82
1912	E Lemming	Sweden	60.64
1920	J Myyra	Finland	65.78
1924	J Myyra	Finland	62.96
1928	E Lundlvist	Finland	66.60
1932	M Jarvinen	Finland	72.70
1936	G Stock	Germany	71.84
1948	K Rautavaara	Finland	69.76

1952	C Young	US	73.78
1956	E Danielsen	Norway	85.70
1960	V Tsibulenko	USSR	84.64
1964	P L Nevala	Finland	82.66
1968	J Lusis	USSR	90.10
1972	K Wolfermann	WGermany	90.48
1976	M Nemeth	Hungary	94.58
1980	D Kula	USSR	91.20

Pentathlon

1912	F Bie	Norway *
1920	E Lehtonen	Norway
1924	E Lehtonen	Norway

* J Thorpe (US) 1st subsequently barred (reinstated 1983)

Decathlon

			points
1912	H Wieslander	Sweden	6161 *
1920	H Loveland	Norway	5970
1924	H Osborn	US	6668
1928	P Yrjola	Finland	6774
1932	J Bausch	US	6896
1936	G Morris	US	7421
1948	R Mathias	US	6825
1952	R Mathias	US	7731
1956	M Campbell	US	7708
1960	R Johnson	US	8001
1964	W Holdorf	Germany	7887
1968	W Toomey	US	8193
1972	N Avilov	USSR	8456 **
1976	B Jenner	US	8617 **
1980	D Thompson	GB	8495 **

* J Thorpe (US) 1st with 6756 subsequently barred (reinstated 1983)

** scored on 1977 revised tables

3,000 metres walk

			min	sec
1920	U Frigerio	Italy	13	14.2

3,500 metres walk

			min	sec
1908	G Larner	GB	14	55.0

10,000 metres walk

			min	sec
1912	G Goulding	Canada	46	28.4
1920	U Frigerio	Italy	48	06.2
1924	U Frigerio	Italy	47	49.0
1948	J F Mikaelsson	Sweden	45	13.2
1952	J F Mikaelsson	Sweden	45	02.8

10 miles walk

			hr	min	sec
1908	G Larner	GB	1	15	57.4

20,000 metres walk			hr	min	sec
1956	L Spirin	USSR	1	31	27.4
1960	V Golubnichiy	USSR	1	34	07.2
1964	K J Matthews	GB	1	29	34.0
1968	V Golubnichiy	USSR	1	33	58.4
1972	P Frenkel	E Germany	1	26	42.4
1976	D Bautista	Mexico	1	24	40.6
1980	M Damilano	Italy	1	23	35.5

50,000 metres walk			hr	min	sec
1932	T W Green	GB	4	50	10.0
1936	H H Whitlock	GB	4	30	41.4
1948	J Ljunggren	Sweden	4	41	52.0
1952	G Dordoni	Italy	4	28	07.8
1956	N Read	New Zealand	4	30	42.8
1960	D J Thompson	GB	4	25	30.0
1964	A Pamich	Italy	4	11	12.4
1968	C Hohne	E Germany	4	20	13.6
1972	B Kannenberg	W Germany	3	56	11.6
1976	not held				
1980	H Gauder	E Germany	3	49	24.0

WOMEN

100 metres			sec
1928	E Robinson	US	12.2
1932	S Walasiewicz	Poland	11.9
1936	H Stephens	US	11.5
1948	F Blankers-Koen	Netherlands	11.9
1952	M Jackson	Australia	11.65
1956	B Cuthbert	Australia	11.82
1960	W Rudolph	US	11.18
1964	W Tyus	US	11.4
1968	W Tyus	US	11.08
1972	R Stecher	E Germany	11.07
1976	A Richter	W Germany	11.08
1980	L Kondratyeva	USSR	11.06

200 metres			sec
1948	F Blankers-Koen	Netherlands	24.4
1952	M Jackson	Australia	23.89
1956	B Cuthbert	Australia	23.55
1960	W Rudolph	US	24.13
1964	E McGuire	US	23.0
1968	I Szewinska	Poland	22.58
1972	R Stecher	E Germany	22.40
1976	B Wockel	E Germany	22.37
1980	B Wockel	E Germany	22.03

400 metres

			sec
1964	B Cuthbert	Australia	52.0
1968	C Besson	France	52.03
1972	M Zehrt	E Germany	51.08
1976	I Szewinska	Poland	49.29
1980	M Koch	E Germany	48.88

800 metres

			min	sec
1928	L Radke	Germany	2	16.8
1960	L Lysenko	USSR	2	04.3
1964	A Packer	GB	2	01.1
1968	M Manning	US	2	00.9
1972	H Falck	W Germany	1	58.6
1976	T Kazankina	USSR	1	54.9
1980	N Olizaryenko	USSR	1	53.5

1500 metres

			min	sec
1972	L Bragina	USSR	4	01.4
1976	T Kazankina	USSR	4	05.5
1980	T Kazankina	USSR	3	56.6

80 metres hurdles

			sec
1932	M Didrikson	US	11.7
1936	T Valla	Italy	11.7
1948	F Blankers-Koen	Netherlands	11.2
1952	S De La Hunty	Australia	11.03
1956	S De La Hunty	Australia	10.96
1960	I Press	USSR	10.94
1964	K Balzer	Germany	10.5
1968	M Caird	Australia	10.3

100 metres hurdles

			sec
1972	A Ehrhardt	E Germany	12.59
1976	J Schaller	E Germany	12.77
1980	V Komissova	USSR	12.56

4×100 metres relay

		sec
1928	Canada	48.4
1932	USA	47.0
1936	USA	46.9
1948	Netherlands	47.5
1952	USA	46.14
1956	Australia	44.65
1960	USA	44.72
1964	Poland	43.6
1968	USA	42.87
1972	West Germany	42.81
1976	East Germany	42.55
1980	East Germany	41.60

4×400 metres relay			min	sec
1972	East Germany		3	23.0
1976	East Germany		3	19.2
1980	USSR		3	20.2

High jump			metres
1928	E Catherwood	Canada	1.59
1932	J Shiley	US	1.65
1936	I Csak	Hungary	1.60
1948	A Coachman	US	1.68
1952	E Brand	South Africa	1.67
1956	M McDaniel	US	1.76
1960	I Balas	Rumania	1.85
1964	I Balas	Rumania	1.90
1968	M Rezkova	Czech	1.82
1972	U Meyfarth	W Germany	1.92
1976	R Ackermann	E Germany	1.93
1980	S Simeoni	Italy	1.97

Long jump			metres
1948	V Gyarmati	Hungary	5.69
1952	Y Williams	New Zealand	6.24
1956	E Krzesinska	Poland	6.35
1960	V Krepkina	USSR	6.37
1964	M Rand	GB	6.76
1968	V Viscopoleanu	Rumania	6.82
1972	H Rosendahl	W Germany	6.78
1976	A Voigt	E Germany	6.72
1980	T Kolpakova	USSR	7.06

Shot			metres
1948	M Ostermeyer	France	13.75
1952	G Zybina	USSR	15.28
1956	T Tyshkevich	USSR	16.59
1960	T Press	USSR	17.32
1964	T Press	USSR	18.14
1968	M Gummel	E Germany	19.61
1972	N Chizhova	USSR	21.03
1976	I Khristova	Bulgaria	21.16
1980	I Slupianek	E Germany	22.41

Discus			metres
1928	H Konopacka	Poland	39.62
1932	L Copeland	US	40.58
1936	G Mauermayer	Germany	47.62
1948	M Ostermeyer	France	41.92
1952	N Ponomaryeva	USSR	51.42
1956	O Fitotova	Czech	53.68
1960	N Ponomaryeva	USSR	55.10
1964	T Press	USSR	57.26

1968	L Manoliu	Rumania	58.28
1972	F Melnik	USSR	66.62
1976	E Jahl	E Germany	69.00
1980	E Jahl	E Germany	69.96

Javelin

			metres
1932	M Didrikson	US	43.68
1936	T Fleischer	Germany	45.18
1948	H Bauma	Austria	45.56
1952	D Zatopkova	Czech	50.46
1956	I Jaunzeme	USSR	53.86
1960	E Ozolina	USSR	55.98
1964	M Penes	Rumania	60.54
1968	A Nemeth	Hungary	60.36
1972	R Fuchs	E Germany	63.88
1976	R Fuchs	E Germany	65.94
1980	M Colon	Cuba	68.40

Pentathlon

			points	
1964	I Press	USSR	5246	
1968	I Mickler	W Germany	5098	
1972	M Peters	GB	4801	*
1976	S Siegl	E Germany	4745	*
1980	N Tkachenko	USSR	5083	**

    * scored on 1970 tables
    ** including 800 metres

WORLD CHAMPIONSHIPS

Venue
1983 Helsinki

MEN

100 metres			**sec**	
C Lewis	USA		10.07	
200 metres			**sec**	
C Smith	USA		20.14	
400 metres			**sec**	
B Cameron	Jamaica		45.05	
800 metres		**min**	**sec**	
W Wuelbeck	W Germany	1	43.05	
1500 metres		**min**	**sec**	
S Cram	GB	3	41.59	

5000 metres			min	sec
E Coghlan	Eire		13	28.53
10,000 metres			min	sec
A Cova	Italy		28	01.04
Marathon		hr	min	sec
R De Castella	Australia	2	10	03
3000 metres steeplechase			min	sec
P Ilg	W Germany		8	15.06
110 metres hurdles				sec
G Foster	USA			13.42
400 metres hurdles				sec
E Moses	USA			47.50
4×100 metres relay				sec
United States				37.86
4×400 metres relay			min	sec
USSR			3	00.79
High jump				metres
G Avdeenko	USSR			2.32
Pole vault				metres
S Bubka	USSR			5.70
Long jump				metres
C Lewis	USA			8.55
Triple jump				metres
Z Hoffman	Poland			17.42
Shot				metres
E Sarul	Poland			21.39
Discus				metres
I Bugar	Czech			67.72
Hammer				metres
S Litvinov	USSR			82.68
Javelin				metres
D Michel	E Germany			89.48
Decathlon				points
D Thompson	GB			8666
20 kilometre walk		hr	min	sec
E Canto	Mexico	1	20	49
50 kilometre walk		hr	min	sec
R Weigal	E Germany	3	43	08

WOMEN

100 metres				sec
M Gohr	E Germany			10.97

200 metres				sec
M Koch	E Germany			22.13

400 metres				sec
J Kratochvilova	Czech			47.99

800 metres			min	sec
J Kratochvilova	Czech		1	54.68

1500 metres			min	sec
M Decker	USA		4	00.90

3000 metres			min	sec
M Decker	USA		8	34.62

Marathon		hr	min	sec
G Waitz	Norway	2	28	09

100 metres hurdles				sec
B Jahn	E Germany			12.35

400 metres hurdles				sec
E Fesenko	USSR			54.14

4×100 metres relay				sec
E Germany				41.76

4×400 metres relay			min	sec
E Germany			3	19.73

High jump		metres
T Bykova	USSR	2.01

Long jump		metres
H Daute	E Germany	7.27

Shot		metres
H Fibingerova	Czech	21.05

Discus		metres
M Opitz	E Germany	68.94

Javelin		metres
T Lillak	Finland	70.82

Heptathlon		points
R Neubert	E Germany	6714

COMMONWEALTH GAMES

Venues

British Empire Games		Commonwealth Games	
1930	Hamilton, Canada	1962	Perth, Australia
1934	London	1966	Kingston, Jamaica
1938	Sydney	1970	Edinburgh
1950	Auckland	1974	Christchurch
1954	Vancouver	1978	Edmonton, Alberta
1958	Cardiff	1982	Brisbane

games accepted metric measurement in 1970

MEN

100 yards

			sec
1930	P Williams	Canada	9.9
1934	A Sweeney	England	10.0
1938	A Holmes	England	9.7
1950	J Treloar	Australia	9.7
1954	M Agostini	Trinidad	9.6
1958	K St H Gardner	Jamaica	9.4
1962	S Antao	Kenya	9.5
1966	H Jerome	Canada	9.4

100 metres

1970	D Quarrie	Jamaica	10.2
1974	D Quarrie	Jamacia	10.38
1978	D Quarrie	Jamaica	10.03
1982	A Wells	Scotland	10.02

220 yards

			sec
1930	S Englehart	England	21.8
1934	A Sweeney	England	21.9
1938	C Holmes	England	21.2
1950	J Treloar	Australia	21.5
1954	D Jowett	New Zealand	21.5
1958	T Robinson	Bahamas	21.0
1962	S Antoa	Kenya	21.1
1966	S Allotey	Ghana	20.7

200 metres

1970	D Quarrie	Jamaica	20.5
1974	D Quarrie	Jamaica	20.73
1978	A Wells	Scotland	20.12
1982	M Macfarlane	England	20.43
	A Wells	Scotland	

440 yards

			sec
1930	A Wilson	Canada	48.8
1934	G Rampling	England	48.0

1938	W Roberts	England		47.9
1950	E Carr	Australia		47.9
1954	R Gosper	Australia		47.2
1958	Milkha Singh	India		46.6
1962	G Kerr	Jamaica		46.7
1966	W Mottley	Trinidad		45.0
400 metres				
1970	C Asati	Kenya		45.0
1974	C Asati	Kenya		46.04
1978	R Mitchell	Australia		46.34
1982	B Cameron	Jamaica		45.89

880 yards			min	sec
1930	T Hampson	England	1	52.4
1934	P Edwards	British Guiana	1	54.2
1938	V Boot	New Zealand	1	51.2
1950	H Parlett	England	1	53.1
1954	D Johnson	England	1	50.7
1958	H Elliott	Australia	1	49.3
1962	P Snell	New Zealand	1	47.6
1966	N Clough	Australia	1	46.4
800 metres				
1970	R Ouko	Kenya	1	46.8
1974	J Kipkurgat	Kenya	1	43.9
1978	M Boit	Kenya	1	46.4
1982	P Bourke	Australia	1	45.18

Mile			min	sec
1930	R Thomas	England	4	14.0
1934	J Lovelock	New Zealand	4	12.8
1938	J Alford	Wales	4	11.6
1950	C Parnell	Canada	4	11.0
1954	R Bannister	England	3	58.8
1958	H Elliott	Australia	3	59.0
1962	P Snell	New Zealand	4	04.6
1966	K Keino	Kenya	3	55.3
1500 metres				
1970	K Keino	Kenya	3	36.6
1974	F Bayi	Tanzania	3	32.2
1978	D Moorcroft	England	3	35.5
1982	S Cram	England	3	42.37

3 miles			min	sec
1930	S Tomlin	England	14	27.4
1934	W Beavers	England	14	32.6
1938	C Matthews	New Zealand	13	59.6
1950	L Eyre	England	14	23.6
1954	C Chataway	England	13	35.2
1958	M Halberg	New Zealand	13	15.0

1962	M Halberg	New Zealand		13	34.2
1966	K Keino	Kenya		12	57.4

5000 metres

1970	I Stewart	Scotland		13	22.8
1974	B Jipcho	Kenya		13	14.4
1978	H Rono	Kenya		13	23.0
1982	D Moorcroft	England		13	33.0

6 miles				**min**	**sec**
1930	W Savidan	New Zealand		30	49.6
1934	A Penny	England		31	00.6
1938	C Matthews	New Zealand		30	14.5
1950	W Nelson	New Zealand		30	29.6
1954	P Driver	England		29	09.4
1958	W Power	Australia		28	47.8
1962	B Kidd	Canada		28	26.6
1966	N Temu	Kenya		27	14.6

10,000 metres

1970	J Stewart	Scotland		28	11.8
1974	R Tayler	New Zealand		27	46.4
1978	B Foster	England		28	13.7
1982	G Shahanga	Tanzania		28	10.15

Marathon			**hr**	**min**	**sec**
1930	D McL Wright	Scotland	2	43	43.0
1934	H Webster	Canada	2	40	36.0
1938	J Coleman	South Africa	2	30	49.8
1950	J Holden	England	2	32	57.0
1954	J McGhee	Scotland	2	39	36.0
1958	W Power	Australia	2	22	45.6
1962	B Kilby	England	2	21	17.0
1966	J Alder	Scotland	2	22	07.8
1970	R Hill	England	2	09	28.0
1974	I Thompson	England	2	09	12.0
1978	G Shahanga	Tanzania	2	15	39.8
1982	R de Castella	Australia	2	09	18.0

Steeplechase				**min**	**sec**
1930 *	G Bailey	England		9	52.0
1934 †	S Scarsbrook	England		10	23.4

3000 metres steeplechase

1962	T Vincent	Australia		8	43.4
1966	R Welsh	New Zealand		8	29.6
1970	A Manning	Australia		8	26.2
1974	B Jipcho	Kenya		8	20.8
1978	H Rono	Kenya		8	26.5
1982	J Korir	Kenya		8	23.94

* ''8 laps'' † 2 miles

120 yards hurdles

			sec
1930	Lord Burghley	England	14.6
1934	D Finlay	England	15.2
1938	T Lavery	South Africa	14.0
1950	P Gardner	Australia	14.3
1954	K St H Gardner	Jamaica	14.2
1958	K St H Gardner	Jamaica	14.0
1962	H Raziq	Pakistan	14.3
1966	D Hemery	England	14.1

110 metres hurdles

1970	D Hemery	England	13.6
1974	F Kimaiyo	Kenya	13.69
1978	B Price	Wales	13.70
1982	M McKoy	Canada	13.37

440 yards hurdles

			sec
1930	Lord Burghley	England	54.4
1934	F Hunter	Scotland	55.2
1938	J Loaring	Canada	52.9
1950	D White	Ceylon	52.5
1954	D Lean	Australia	52.4
1958	G Potgieter	South Africa	49.7
1962	K Roche	Australia	51.5
1966	K Roche	Australia	51.0

400 metres hurdles

1970	J Sherwood	England	50.0
1974	A Pascoe	England	48.83
1978	D Kimaiyo	Kenya	49.49
1982	G Brown	Australia	49.37

4 × 110 yards relay

		sec
1930	Canada	42.2
1934	England	42.2
1938	Canada	41.6
1950	Australia	42.2
1954	Canada	41.3
1958	England	40.7
1962	England	40.6
1966	Ghana	39.8

4 × 100 metres relay

		sec
1970	Jamaica	39.4
1974	Australia	39.3
1978	Scotland	39.24
1982	Nigeria	39.15

4 × 440 yards relay

		min	sec
1930	England	3	19.4
1934	England	3	16.8
1938	Canada	3	16.9
1950	Australia	3	17.8
1954	England	3	11.2
1958	South Africa	3	08.1
1962	Jamaica	3	10.2
1966	Trinidad and Tobago	3	02.8

4 × 400 metres relay			min	sec
1970	Kenya		3	03.6
1974	Kenya		3	04.4
1978	Kenya		3	03.5
1982	England		3	05.45

High jump			metres
1930	J Viljoen	South Africa	1.90
1934	E Thacker	South Africa	1.90
1938	E Thacker	South Africa	1.95
1950	J Winter	Australia	1.98
1954	E Ifeajuna	Nigeria	2.03
1958	E Haisley	Jamaica	2.05
1962	P Hobson	Australia	2.11
1966	L Peckham	Australia	2.08
1970	L Peckham	Australia	2.14
1974	G Windeyer	Australia	2.16
1978	C Ferragne	Canada	2.20
1982	M Ottey	Canada	2.31

Pole vault			metres
1930	V Pickard	Canada	3.37
1934	C Apps	Canada	3.81
1938	A du Plessis	South Africa	4.11
1950	T Anderson	England	3.96
1954	G Elliott	England	4.26
1958	G Elliott	England	4.16
1962	T Bickle	Australia	4.49
1966	T Bickle	Australia	4.80
1970	M Bull	N Ireland	5.10
1974	D Baird	Australia	5.05
1978	B Simpson	Canada	5.10
1982	R Boyd	Australia	5.20

Long jump			metres
1930	L Hutton	Canada	7.20
1934	S Richardson	Canada	7.17
1938	H Brown	Canada	7.43
1950	N Price	South Africa	7.31
1954	K Wilmshurst	England	7.54
1958	P Foreman	Jamaica	7.47
1962	M Ahey	Ghana	8.05
1966	L Davies	Wales	7.99
1970	L Davies	Wales	8.06
1974	A Lerwill	England	7.94
1978	R Mitchell	England	8.06
1982	G Honey	Australia	8.13

Triple jump			metres
1930	G Smallacombe	Canada	14.76
1934	J Metcalfe	Australia	15.63
1938	J Metcalfe	Australia	15.49
1950	B T Oliver	Australia	15.61
1954	K Wilmshurst	England	15.28
1958	I Tomlinson	Australia	15.73
1962	I Tomlinson	Australia	16.20
1966	S Igun	Nigeria	16.40
1970	P May	Australia	16.72
1974	J Owusu	Ghana	16.50
1978	K Connor	England	17.21
1982	K Connor	England	17.81

Shot			metres
1930	H Hart	South Africa	14.58
1934	H Hart	South Africa	14.67
1938	L Fouche	South Africa	14.48
1950	M Tuicakau	Fiji	14.63
1954	J Savidge	England	16.77
1958	A Rowe	England	17.57
1962	M Lucking	England	18.08
1966	D Steen	Canada	18.79
1970	D Steen	Canada	19.21
1974	G Capes	England	20.74
1978	G Capes	England	19.77
1982	B Pauletto	Canada	19.55

Discus			metres
1930	H Hart	South Africa	41.44
1934	H Hart	South Africa	41.54
1938	E Coy	Canada	44.76
1950	I Reed	Australia	47.72
1954	S du Plessis	South Africa	51.70
1958	S du Plessis	South Africa	55.94
1962	W Selvey	Australia	56.48
1966	L Mills	New Zealand	56.18
1970	G Puce	Canada	59.04
1974	R Tait	New Zealand	63.08
1978	B Chanbul	Canada	59.70
1982	B Cooper	Bahamas	64.04

Hammer			metres
1930	M Nokes	England	47.12
1934	M Nokes	England	48.24
1938	G Sutherland	Scotland	48.72
1950	D McD Clark	Scotland	49.94
1954	M Iqbal	Pakistan	55.38
1958	M Ellis	England	62.90

1962	H Payne	England	61.64
1966	H Payne	England	61.98
1970	H Payne	England	67.80
1974	I Chipchase	England	69.56
1978	P Farmer	Australia	71.10
1982	R Weir	England	75.08

Javelin

			metres
1930	S Lay	New Zealand	63.12
1934	R Dixon	Canada	60.02
1938	J Courtwright	Canada	62.82
1950	L Roininen	Canada	57.10
1954	J Adchurch	Australia	68.52
1958	C Smith	England	71.28
1962	A Mitchell	Australia	78.10
1966	J Fitzsimmons	England	79.78
1970	D Travis	England	79.50
1974	C Clover	England	84.92
1978	P Olsen	Canada	84.00
1982	M O'Rourke	New Zealand	89.48

Decathlon

			points
1966	R Williams	New Zealand	7270
1970	G Smith	Australia	7492
1974	M Bull	N Ireland	7417
1978	D Thompson	England	8467
1982	D Thompson	England	8410

20 miles walk

			hr	min	sec
1966	R Wallwork	England	2	44	42.8
1970	N Freeman	Australia	2	33	33.0
1974	J Warhurst	England	2	35	23.0

30 km walk

			hr	min	sec
1978	O Flynn	England	2	22	03.7
1982	S Barry	Wales	2	10	16.0

WOMEN

100 yards

			sec
1934	E Hiscock	England	11.3
1938	D Norman	Australia	11.1
1950	M Nelson	Australia	10.8
1954	M Nelson	Australia	10.7
1958	M Willard	Australia	10.6
1962	D Hyman	England	11.2
1966	D Burge	Australia	10.6

100 metres

1970	R Boyle	Australia	11.2
1974	R Boyle	Australia	11.27
1978	S Lannaman	England	10.6
1982	A Taylor	Canada	11.0

220 yards

			sec
934	E Hiscock	England	25.0
1938	D Norman	Australia	24.7
1950	M Nelson	Australia	24.3
1954	M Nelson	Australia	24.0
1958	M Willard	Australia	23.6
1962	D Hyman	England	23.8
1966	D Burge	Australia	23.8

200 metres

1970	R Boyle	Australia	22.7
1974	R Boyle	Australia	22.50
1978	D Boyd	Australia	22.82
1982	M Ottey	Jamaica	22.19

440 yards

			sec
1966	J Pollock	Australia	53.0

400 metres

1970	M Neufville	Jamaica	51.0
1974	Y Saunders	Canada	51.67
1978	D Hartley	England	51.69
1982	R Boyle	Australia	51.26

880 yards

			min	**sec**
1934	G Lunn	England	2	19.4
1962	D Willis	Australia	2	03.7
1966	A Hoffman	Canada	2	04.3

800 metres

1970	R Stirling	Scotland	2	06.2
1974	C Rendina	Australia	2	01.1
1978	J Peckham	Australia	2	02.8
1982	K McDermott	Wales	2	01.31

1500 metres

			min	**sec**
1970	R Ridley	England	4	18.8
1974	G Reiser	Canada	4	07.8
1978	M Stewart	England	4	06.3
1982	C Boxer	England	4	08.28

3000 metres

			min	**sec**
1978	P Fudge	England	9	13.0
1982	A Audain	New Zealand	8	45.53

80 yards hurdles			sec
1934	M Clarke	South Africa	11.8
1938	B Burke	South Africa	11.7
1950	S Strickland	Australia	11.6
1954	E Maskell	Rhodesia	10.9
1958	N Thrower	Australia	10.7
1962	P Kilborn	Australia	10.9
1966	P Kilborn	Australia	10.9
100 metres hurdles			
1970	P Kilborn	Australia	13.2
1974	J Vernon	England	13.45
1978	L Boothe	England	12.98
1982	S Strong	England	12.78

400 metres hurdles			sec
1982	D Flintoff	Australia	55.89

110+220+110 yards relay		sec
1934	England	49.4
1938	Australia	49.1
1950	Australia	47.9
4×110 yards relay		
1954	Australia	46.8
1958	England	45.3
1962	Australia	46.6
1966	Australia	45.3
4×100 metres relay		
1970	Australia	44.1
1974	Australia	43.51
1978	England	43.51
1982	England	43.15

220+110+220+110 yards relay		min	sec
1934	Canada	1	14.4
1938	Australia	1	15.2
1950	Australia	1	13.4

4×400 metres relay		min	sec
1974	England	3	29.2
1978	England	3	27.2
1982	Canada	3	27.70

High jump			metres
1934	M Clarke	South Africa	1.60
1938	D Tyler	England	1.60
1950	D Tyler	England	1.60
1954	T Hopkins	N Ireland	1.67
1958	M Brown	Australia	1.70
1962	R Woodhouse	Australia	1.78
1966	M Brown	Australia	1.72
1970	D Brill	Canada	1.78
1974	B Lawton	England	1.84
1978	K Gibbs	Australia	1.93
1982	D Brill	Canada	1.88

Long jump			metres
1934	P Bartholomew	England	5.47
1938	D Norman	Australia	5.80
1950	Y Williams	New Zealand	5.90

1954	Y Williams	New Zealand	6.08
1958	S Hoskins	England	6.02
1962	P Kilborn	Australia	6.27
1966	M Rand	England	6.36
1970	S Sherwood	England	6.73
1974	M Oshikoya	Nigeria	6.46
1978	S Reeves	England	6.59
1982	S Ferguson	Bahamas	6.91

Shot

			metres
1954	Y Williams	New Zealand	13.96
1958	V Young	New Zealand	15.54
1962	V Young	New Zealand	15.23
1966	V Young	New Zealand	16.50
1970	M Peters	N Ireland	15.93
1974	J Haist	Canada	16.12
1978	G Mulhall	Australia	17.31
1982	J Oakes	England	17.92

Discus

			metres
1954	Y Williams	New Zealand	45.02
1958	S Allday	England	45.90
1962	V Young	New Zealand	50.20
1966	V Young	New Zealand	49.78
1970	R Payne	Scotland	54.46
1974	J Haist	Canada	55.52
1978	C Ionesco	Canada	62.16
1982	M Ritchie	Scotland	62.98

Javelin

			metres
1934	G Lunn	England	32.18
1938	R Higgins	Canada	38.28
1950	C McGibbon	Australia	38.84
1954	M Swanepoel	South Africa	43.82
1958	A Pazera	Australia	57.40
1962	S Platt	England	50.24
1966	M Parker	Australia	51.38
1970	P Rivers	Australia	52.00
1974	P Rivers	Australia	55.48
1978	T Sanderson	England	61.34
1982	S Howland	Australia	64.46

Pentathlon

			points
1970	M Peters	N Ireland	4524
1974	M Peters	N Ireland	4455
1978	D Konihowski	Canada	4768

Heptathlon

			points
1982	G Nunn	Australia	6282

EUROPEAN CHAMPIONSHIPS

Venues

1934	Turin (men only)	1962	Belgrade
1938	Paris (men)	1966	Budapest
	Vienna (women)	1969	Athens
1946	Oslo	1971	Helsinki
1950	Brussels	1974	Rome
1954	Berne	1978	Prague
1958	Stockholm	1982	Athens

MEN

100 metres

			sec
1934	C Berger	Netherlands	10.6
1938	M Osendarp	Netherlands	10.5
1946	J Archer	GB	10.6
1950	E Bally	France	10.7
1954	H Futterer	Germany	10.5
1958	A Hary	Germany	10.3
1962	C Piquemal	France	10.4
1966	W Maniak	Poland	10.5
1969	V Borzov	USSR	10.4
1971	V Borzov	USSR	10.26
1974	V Borzov	USSR	10.27
1978	P Mennea	Italy	10.27
1982	F Emmelmann	E Germany	10.21

200 metres

			sec
1934	C Berger	Netherlands	21.5
1938	M Osendarp	Netherlands	21.2
1946	N Karakulov	USSR	21.6
1950	B Shenton	GB	21.5
1954	H Futterer	Germany	20.9
1958	M Germar	Germany	21.0
1962	O Jonsson	Sweden	20.7
1966	R Bambuck	France	20.9
1969	P Clerc	Switzerland	20.6
1971	V Borzov	USSR	20.30
1974	P Mennea	Italy	20.60
1978	P Mennea	Italy	20.16
1982	O Prenzler	E Germany	20.46

400 metres

			sec
1934	A Metzner	Germany	47.9
1938	A Brown	GB	47.4
1946	N Holst Sorensen	Denmark	47.9

1950	D Pugh	GB	47.3
1954	A Ignatyev	USSR	46.6
1958	J Wrighton	GB	46.3
1962	R Brightwell	GB	45.9
1966	S Gredzinski	Poland	46.0
1969	J Werner	Poland	45.7
1971	D Jenkins	GB	45.45
1974	K Honz	W Germany	45.04
1978	F-P Hofmeister	W Germany	45.73
1982	H Weber	W Germany	44.72

800 metres

			min	sec
1934	M Szabo	Hungary	1	52.0
1938	R Harbig	Germany	1	50.6
1946	R Gustafsson	Sweden	1	51.0
1950	H Parlett	GB	1	50.5
1954	L Szentgali	Hungary	1	47.1
1958	M Rawson	GB	1	47.8
1962	M Matuschewski	Germany	1	50.5
1966	M Matuschewski	Germany	1	45.9
1969	D Fromm	E Germany	1	45.9
1971	Y Arzhanov	USSR	1	45.6
1974	L Susanj	Yugoslavia	1	44.1
1978	O Beyer	E Germany	1	43.8
1982	H-P Ferner	W Germany	1	46.33

1500 metres

			min	sec
1934	L Beccali	Italy	3	54.6
1938	S Wooderson	GB	3	53.6
1946	L Strand	Sweden	3	48.0
1950	W Slijkhuis	Netherlands	3	47.2
1954	R Bannister	GB	3	43.8
1958	B Hewson	GB	3	41.9
1962	M Jazy	France	3	40.9
1966	B Tummler	W Germany	3	41.9
1969	J Whetton	GB	3	39.4
1971	F Arese	Italy	3	38.4
1974	K Justus	E Germany	3	40.6
1978	S Ovett	GB	3	35.6
1982	S Cram	GB	3	36.49

5000 metres

			min	sec
1934	R Rochard	France	14	36.8
1938	T Maki	Finland	14	26.8
1946	S Wooderson	GB	14	08.6
1950	E Zatopek	Czech	14	03.0
1954	V Kuts	USSR	13	56.6
1958	Z Krzyszkowiak	Poland	13	53.4
1962	B Tulloch	GB	14	00.6

1966	M Jazy	France	13	42.8
1969	I Stewart	GB	13	44.8
1971	J Vaatainen	Finland	13	32.6
1974	B Foster	GB	13	17.2
1978	V Ortis	Italy	13	28.5
1982	T Wessinghage	W Germany	13	28.90

10,000 metres

			min	sec
1934	I Salminen	Finland	31	02.6
1938	I Salminen	Finland	30	52.4
1946	V Heino	Finland	29	52.0
1950	E Zatopek	Czech	29	12.0
1954	E Zatopek	Czech	28	58.0
1958	Z Krzyszkowiak	Poland	28	56.0
1962	P Bolotnikov	USSR	28	54.0
1966	J Haase	E Germany	28	26.0
1969	J Haase	E Germany	28	41.6
1971	J Vaatainen	Finland	27	52.8
1974	M Kuschmann	E Germany	28	25.8
1978	M Vainio	Finland	27	31.0
1982	A Cova	Italy	27	41.03

Marathon

			hr	min	sec
1934	A Toivonen	Finland	2	52	29.0
1938	V Muinonen	Finland	2	37	28.8
1946	M Hietanen	Finland	2	24	55.0 *
1950	J Holden	GB	2	32	13.2
1954	V Karvonen	Finland	2	24	51.6
1958	S Popov	USSR	2	15	17.0
1962	B Kilby	GB	2	23	18.8
1966	J Hogan	GB	2	20	04.6
1969	R Hill	GB	2	16	47.8
1971	K Lismont	Belgium	2	13	09.9
1974	I Thompson	GB	2	13	18.8
1978	L Moseyev	USSR	2	11	57.5
1982	G Nijboer	Netherlands	2	15	16.0

* short course

3000 metres steeplechase

			min	sec
1938	L Larsson	Sweden	9	16.2
1946	R Pujazon	France	9	01.4
1950	J Roudny	Czech	9	05.4
1954	S Rozsnyoi	Hungary	8	49.6
1958	J Chromik	Poland	8	38.2
1962	G Roelants	Belgium	8	32.6
1966	V Kudinskiy	USSR	8	26.6
1969	M Zhelev	Bulgaria	8	25.0
1971	J-P Villain	France	8	25.2
1974	B Malinowski	Poland	8	15.0

| 1978 | B Malinowski | Poland | 8 | 15.1 |
| 1982 | P Ilg | W Germany | 8 | 18.52 |

110 metres hurdles

			sec
1934	J Kovacs	Hungary	14.8
1938	D Finlay	GB	14.3
1946	E Lidman	Sweden	14.6
1950	A Marie	France	14.6
1954	Y Bulanchik	USSR	14.4
1958	K Lauer	Germany	13.7
1962	A Mikhailov	USSR	13.8
1966	E Ottoz	Italy	13.7
1969	E Ottoz	Italy	13.5
1971	F Siebek	E Germany	14.0
1974	G Drut	France	13.40
1978	T Munkelt	E Germany	13.54
1982	T Munkelt	E Germany	13.41

400 metres hurdles

			sec
1934	H Scheele	Germany	53.2
1938	P Joyce	France	53.1
1946	B Storskrubb	Finland	52.2
1950	A Filiput	Italy	51.9
1954	A Yulin	USSR	50.5
1958	Y Lituyev	USSR	51.1
1962	S Morale	Italy	49.2
1966	R Frinolli	Italy	49.8
1969	V Skomorokhov	USSR	49.7
1971	J-C Nallet	France	49.2
1974	A Pascoe	GB	48.82
1978	H Schmid	W Germany	48.51
1982	H Schmid	W Germany	47.48

4×100 metres relay sec

			sec			
1934	Germany	41.0		1966	France	39.4
1938	Germany	40.9		1969	France	38.8
1946	Sweden	41.5		1971	Czechoslovakia	39.3
1950	USSR	41.5		1974	France	38.69
1954	Hungary	40.6		1978	Poland	38.58
1958	Germany	40.2		1982	USSR	38.60
1962	Germany	39.5				

4×400 metres relay min sec

			min sec				min sec
1934	Germany	3	14.1	1966	Poland	3	04.5
1938	Germany	3	13.7	1969	France	3	02.3
1946	France	3	14.4	1971	W Germany	3	02.9
1950	Great Britain	3	10.2	1974	Great Britain	3	03.3
1954	France	3	08.8*	1978	W Germany	3	02.0
1958	Great Britain	3	07.9	1982	W Germany	3	00.51
1962	Germany	3	05.8	* GB 1st but disqualified			

High jump

			metres
1934	K Kotkas	Finland	2.00
1938	K Lundqvist	Sweden	1.97
1946	A Bolinder	Sweden	1.99
1950	A Paterson	GB	1.96
1954	B Nilsson	Sweden	2.02
1958	R Dahl	Sweden	2.12
1962	V Brumel	USSR	2.21
1966	J Madubost	France	2.12
1969	V Gavrilov	USSR	2.17
1971	K Sapka	USSR	2.20
1974	J Torring	Denmark	2.25
1978	V Yashchenko	USSR	2.30
1982	D Mogenburg	W Germany	2.30

Pole vault

			metres
1934	G Wegner	Germany	4.0
1938	K Sutter	Germany	4.05
1946	A Lindberg	Sweden	4.17
1950	R Lundberg	Sweden	4.30
1954	E Landstrom	Finland	4.40
1958	E Landstrom	Finland	4.50
1962	P Nikula	Finland	4.80
1966	W Nordwig	E Germany	5.10
1969	W Nordwig	E Germany	5.30
1971	W Nordwig	E Germany	5.35
1974	V Kishkun	USSR	5.35
1978	V Trofimenko	USSR	5.55
1982	A Krupskiy	USSR	5.60

Long jump

			metres
1934	W Leichum	Germany	7.45
1938	W Leichum	Germany	7.65
1946	O Laessker	Sweden	7.42
1950	T Bryngeirsson	Iceland	7.32
1954	O Foldessy	Hungary	7.51
1958	I Ter-Ovanesyan	USSR	7.81
1962	I Ter-Ovanesyan	USSR	8.19
1966	L Davies	GB	7.98
1969	I Ter-Ovanesyan	USSR	8.17
1971	M Klauss	E Germany	7.92
1974	V Podluzhny	USSR	8.12
1978	J Rousseau	France	8.18
1982	L Dombrowski	E Germany	8.41

Triple jump

			metres
1934	W Peters	Netherlands	14.89
1938	O Rajasaari	Finland	15.32
1946	K Rautio	Finland	15.17

1950	L Shcherbakov	USSR	15.39
1954	L Shcherbakov	USSR	15.90
1958	J Szmidt	Poland	16.43
1962	J Szmidt	Poland	16.55
1966	G Stoikovski	Bulgaria	16.67
1969	V Sanyeyev	USSR	17.34
1971	J Drehmel	E Germany	17.16
1974	V Sanyeyev	USSR	17.23
1978	M Srejovic	Yugoslavia	16.94
1982	K Connor	GB	17.29

Shot			metres
1934	A Viiding	Estonia	15.19
1938	A Kreek	Estonia	15.83
1946	G Huseby	Iceland	15.56
1950	G Huseby	Iceland	16.74
1954	J Skobla	Czech	17.20
1958	A Rowe	GB	17.78
1962	V Varju	Hungary	19.02
1966	V Varju	Hungary	19.43
1969	D Hoffmann	E Germany	20.12
1971	H Briesenick	E Germany	21.08
1974	H Briesenick	E Germany	20.50
1978	U Beyer	E Germany	21.08
1982	U Beyer	E Germany	21.50

Discus			metres
1934	H Andersson	Sweden	50.38
1938	W Schroeder	Germany	49.70
1946	A Consolini	Italy	53.22
1950	A Consolini	Italy	53.74
1954	A Consolini	Italy	53.44
1958	E Piatkowski	Poland	53.92
1962	V Trusenyov	USSR	57.10
1966	D Thorith	E Germany	57.42
1969	H Losch	E Germany	61.82
1971	L Danek	Czech	63.90
1974	P Kahma	Finland	63.62
1978	W Schmidt	E Germany	66.82
1982	I Bugar	Czech	66.64

Hammer			metres
1934	V Porhola	Finland	50.34
1938	K Hein	Germany	58.76
1946	B Ericson	Sweden	56.44
1950	S Strandli	Norway	55.70
1954	M Krivonosov	USSR	63.34
1958	T Rut	Poland	64.78
1962	G Zsivotzky	Hungary	69.64

1966	R Klim	USSR	70.02
1969	A Bondarchuk	USSR	74.68
1971	U Beyer	W Germany	72.36
1974	A Spiridonov	USSR	74.20
1978	Y Sedykh	USSR	77.28
1982	Y Sedykh	USSR	81.66

Javelin

			metres
1934	M Jarvinen	Finland	76.66
1938	M Jarvinen	Finland	76.86
1946	A Atterwall	Sweden	68.74
1950	T Hyytiainen	Finland	71.26
1954	J Sidlo	Poland	76.34
1958	J Sidlo	Poland	80.18
1962	J Lusis	USSR	82.04
1966	J Lusis	USSR	84.48
1969	J Lusis	USSR	91.52
1971	J Lusis	USSR	90.68
1974	H Siitonen	Finland	89.58
1978	M Wessing	W Germany	89.12
1982	U Hohn	E Germany	91.34

Decathlon

			points
1934	H Sievert	Germany	6858
1938	O Bexell	Sweden	6870
1946	G Holmvang	Norway	6760
1950	I Heinrich	France	7009
1954	V Kuznyetsov	USSR	7043
1958	V Kuznyetsov	USSR	7697
1962	V Kuznyetsov	USSR	7770
1966	W Von Moltke	W Germany	7740
1969	J Kirst	E Germany	8041
1971	J Kirst	E Germany	8196
1974	R Skowronek	Poland	8207
1978	A Grebenyuk	USSR	8340
1982	D Thompson	GB	8743

10,000 metres walk

			min	sec
1946	J Mikaelsson	Sweden	46	05.2
1950	F Schwab	Switzerland	46	01.8
1954	J Dolezal	Czech	45	01.8

20,000 metres walk

			hr	min	sec
1058	S Vickers	GB	1	33	09.0
1962	K Matthews	GB	1	35	54.8
1966	D Lindner	E Germany	1	29	25.0
1969	P Nihill	GB	1	30	41.0
1971	N Smaga	USSR	1	27	20.2

1974	V Golubnichiy	USSR	1	29	30.0
1978	R Wieser	E Germany	1	23	11.5
1982	J Marin	Spain	1	23	43.0

50,000 metres walk			hr	min	sec
1934	J Dalins	Latvia	4	49	52.6
1938	H Whitlock	GB	4	41	51.0
1946	J Ljunggren	Sweden	4	38	20.0
1950	G Dordoni	Italy	4	40	42.6
1954	V Ukhov	USSR	4	22	11.2
1958	Y Maskinskov	USSR	4	17	15.4
1962	A Pamich	Italy	4	18	46.6
1966	A Pamich	Italy	4	18	42.2
1969	C Hohne	E Germany	4	13	32.8
1971	V Solsatenko	USSR	4	02	22.0
1974	C Hohne	E Germany	3	59	05.6
1978	J Llopart	Spain	3	53	29.9
1982	R Salonen	Finland	3	55	29.0

WOMEN

100 metres			sec
1938	S Walasiewicz	Poland	11.9
1946	Y Sechenova	USSR	11.9
1950	F Blankers-Koen	Netherlands	11.7
1954	I Turova	USSR	11.8
1958	H Young	GB	11.7
1962	D Hyman	GB	11.3
1966	E Klobukowska	Poland	11.5
1969	P Vogt	E Germany	11.6
1971	R Stecher	E Germany	11.35
1974	I Szewinska	Poland	11.13
1978	M Gohr	E Germany	11.13
1982	M Gohr	E Germany	11.01

200 metres			sec
1938	S Walasiewicz	Poland	23.8
1946	Y Sechenova	USSR	25.4
1950	F Blankers-Koen	Netherlands	24.0
1954	M Itkina	USSR	24.3
1958	B Sobotta	Poland	24.1
1962	J Heine	Germany	23.5
1966	I Szewinska	Poland	23.1
1969	P Vogt	E Germany	23.2
1971	R Stecher	E Germany	22.71
1974	I Szewinska	Poland	22.51
1978	L Kondratyeva	USSR	22.52
1982	B Wockel	E Germany	22.04

400 metres

			sec
1958	M Itkina	USSR	53.7
1962	M Itkina	USSR	53.4
1966	A Chmelkova	Czech	52.9
1969	N Duclos	France	51.72
1971	H Seidler	E Germany	52.1
1974	R Salin	Finland	50.14
1978	M Koch	E Germany	48.94
1982	M Koch	E Germany	48.15

800 metres

			min	sec
1954	N Otkalenko	USSR	2	08.8
1958	Y Yermolayeva	USSR	2	06.3
1962	G Kraan	Netherlands	2	02.8
1966	V Nikolic	Yugoslavia	2	02.8
1969	L Board	GB	2	01.4
1971	V Nikolic	Yugoslavia	2	00.0
1974	L Tomova	Bulgaria	1	58.1
1978	T Providokhina	USSR	1	55.8
1982	O Mineyeva	USSR	1	55.41

1500 metres

			min	sec
1969	J Jehlickova	Czech	4	10.7
1971	K Burneleit	E Germany	4	09.6
1974	G Hoffmeister	E Germany	4	02.3
1978	G Romanova	USSR	3	59.0
1982	O Dvirna	USSR	3	57.80

3000 metres

			min	sec
1974	N Holmen	Finland	8	55.2
1978	S Ulmasova	USSR	8	33.2
1982	S Ulmasova	USSR	8	30.28

Marathon

			hr	min	sec
1982	R Mota	Portugal	2	36	04

80 metres hurdles

			sec
1938	C Testoni	Italy	11.6
1946	F Blankers-Koen	Netherlands	11.8
1950	F Blankers-Koen	Netherlands	11.1
1954	M Golubnichaya	USSR	11.0
1958	G Bystrova	USSR	10.9
1962	T Ciepla	Poland	10.6
1966	K Balzer	E Germany	10.7

100 metres hurdles

			sec
1969	K Balzer	E Germany	13.2
1971	K Balzer	E Germany	12.94
1974	A Ehrhardt	E Germany	12.66

1978	J Klier	E Germany	12.62
1982	L Kalek	Poland	12.45

400 metres hurdles

			sec
1978	T Zelentsova	E Germany	54.89
1982	A-L Skoglund	Sweden	54.58

4 × 100 metres relay   sec

		sec			sec
1938	Germany	46.8	1966	Poland	44.4
1946	Netherlands	47.8	1969	E Germany	43.6
1950	Great Britain	47.4	1971	W Germany	43.3
1954	USSR	45.8	1974	E Germany	42.51
1958	USSR	45.3	1978	USSR	42.54
1962	Poland	44.5	1982	E Germany	42.19

4 × 400 metres relay

		min	sec
1969	Great Britain	3	30.8
1971	E Germany	3	29.3
1974	E Germany	3	25.2
1978	E Germany	3	21.2
1982	E Germany	3	19.05

High jump

			metres	
1938	I Csak	Hungary	1.64	*
1946	A Colchen	France	1.60	
1950	S Alexander	GB	1.63	
1954	T Hopkins	GB	1.67	
1958	I Balas	Rumania	1.77	
1962	I Balas	Rumania	1.83	
1966	T Chenchik	USSR	1.75	
1969	M Rezkova	Czech	1.83	
1971	I Gusenbauer	Austria	1.87	
1974	R Witschas	E Germany	1.95	
1978	S Simeoni	Italy	2.01	
1982	U Meyfarth	W Germany	2.02	

* D Ratjen (Germany) 1st but disqualified following sex change

Long jump

			metres
1938	I Praetz	Germany	5.88
1946	G Koudijs	Netherlands	5.67
1950	V Bogdanova	USSR	5.82
1954	J Desforges	GB	6.04
1958	L Jacobi	Germany	6.14
1962	T Shchelkanova	USSR	6.36
1966	I Szewinska	Poland	6.55
1969	M Sarna	Poland	6.49
1971	I Mickler	W Germany	6.76

1974	I Bruzsenyak	Hungary	6.65
1978	V Bardauskiene	USSR	6.88
1982	V Ionescu	Rumania	6.79

Shot | | | metres

1938	H Schroder	Germany	13.29
1946	T Sevryukova	USSR	14.16
1950	A Andreyeva	USSR	14.32
1954	G Zybina	USSR	15.65
1958	M Werner	Germany	15.74
1962	T Press	USSR	18.55
1966	N Chizhova	USSR	17.22
1969	N Chizhova	USSR	20.43
1971	N Chizhova	USSR	20.16
1974	N Chizhova	USSR	20.78
1978	I Slupianek	E Germany	21.41
1982	I Slupianek	E Germany	21.59

Discus | | | metres

1938	G Mauermayer	Germany	44.80
1946	N Dumbadze	USSR	44.52
1950	N Dumbadze	USSR	48.02
1954	N Ponomaryeva	USSR	48.02
1958	T Press	USSR	52.32
1962	T Press	USSR	56.90
1966	C Spielberg	E Germany	57.76
1969	T Danilova	USSR	59.28
1971	F Melnik	USSR	64.22
1974	F Melnik	USSR	69.00
1978	E Jahl	E Germany	66.98
1982	T Hristova	Bulgaria	68.34

Javelin | | | metres

1938	L Gelius	Germany	45.58
1946	K Mayuchaya	USSR	46.24
1950	N Smirnitskaya	USSR	47.57
1954	D Zatopkova	Czech	52.90
1958	D Zatopkova	Czech	56.02
1962	E Ozolina	USSR	54.92
1966	M Luttge	E Germany	58.74
1969	A Ranky	Hungary	59.76
1971	D Jaworska	Poland	61.00
1974	R Fuchs	E Germany	67.22
1978	R Fuchs	E Germany	69.16
1982	A Verouli	Greece	70.02

Pentathlon | | | points

1950	A Ben Hamo	France	3544
1954	A Chudina	USSR	4020
1958	G Bystrova	USSR	4215

1962	G Bystrova	USSR	4312
1966	V Tikhomirova	USSR	4272
1969	L Prokop	Austria	4419
1971	H Rosendahl	W Germany	4675
1974	N Tkachenko	USSR	4776 *
1978	M Papp	Hungary	4655

* Tkachenko disqualified after dope test

Heptathlon			points
1982	R Neubert	E Germany	6622

WORLD CUP

OVERALL TEAM RESULTS

MEN

1977 Dusseldorf

		points
1	E Germany	127
2	USA	120
3	W Germany	112
4	Europe	111
5	Americas	92
6	Africa	78
7	Oceania	48
8	Asia	44

1979 Montreal

1	USA	119
2	Europe	112
3	E Germany	108
4	USSR	102
5	Americas	98
6	Africa	84
7	Oceania	58
8	Asia	36

1981 Rome

1	Europe	139
2	E Germany	126
3	USA	118
4	USSR	112
5	Americas	88
6	Italy	88
7	Africa	63
8	Oceania	59
9	Asia	58

WOMEN

		points
1	Europe	107
2	E Germany	102
3	USSR	89
4	USA	59
5	Americas	55
6	Oceania	45
7	Africa	31
8	Asia	29

1	E Germany	105
2	USSR	97
3	Europe	96
4	USA	75
5	Americas	67
6	Oceania	46
7	Africa	29
8	Asia	25

1	E Germany	120½
2	Europe	110
3	USSR	98
4	USA	89
5	Americas	72
6	Italy	68½
7	Oceania	58
8	Asia	32
9	Africa	26

INDIVIDUAL WINNERS

MEN

100 metres sec

1977	S Williams	USA	10.13
1979	J Sanford	USA	10.17
1981	A Wells	Europe	10.20

200 metres sec

1977	C Edwards	USA	20.17
1979	S Leonard	Americas	20.34
1981	M Lattany	USA	20.21

400 metres sec

1977	A Juantorena	Americas	45.36
1979	H El Kashief	Africa	45.39
1981	C Wiley	USA	44.88

800 metres min sec

1977	A Juantorena	Americas	1	44.0
1979	J Maina	Africa	1	47.7
1981	S Coe	Europe	1	46.16

1500 metres min sec

1977	S Ovett	Europe	3	45.5
1979	T Wessinghage	Europe	3	46.0
1981	S Ovett	Europe	3	34.95

5000 metres min sec

1977	M Yifter	Africa	13	13.8
1979	M Yifter	Africa	13	35.9
1981	E Coghlan	Europe	14	08.39

10,000 metres min sec

1977	M Yifter	Africa	28	32.3
1979	M Yifter	Africa	27	53.1
1981	W Schildhauer	E Germany	27	38.43

3000 metres steeplechase min sec

1977	M Karst	W Germany	8	21.6
1979	K Rono	Africa	8	26.0
1981	B Maminski	Europe	8	19.89

110 metres hurdles

			sec
1977	T Munkelt	E Germany	13.41
1979	R Nehemiah	USA	13.39
1981	G Foster	USA	13.32

400 metres hurdles

			sec
1977	E Moses	USA	47.58
1979	E Moses	USA	47.53
1981	E Moses	USA	47.37

4×100 metres relay

		sec
1977	USA	38.03
1979	Americas	38.70
1981	Europe	38.73

4×400 metres relay

		min	sec
1977	W Germany	3	01.3
1979	USA	3	00.7
1981	USA	2	59.12

High jump

			metres
1977	R Beilschmidt	E Germany	2.30
1979	F Jacobs	USA	2.27
1981	T Peacock	USA	2.28

Pole vault

			metres
1977	M Tully	USA	5.60
1979	M Tully	USA	5.45
1981	K Volkov	USSR	5.70

Long jump

			metres
1977	A Robinson	USA	8.19
1979	L Myricks	USA	8.52
1981	C Lewis	USA	8.15

Triple jump

			metres
1977	C De Oliveria	Americas	16.68
1979	C De Oliveria	Americas	17.02
1981	C De Oliveria	Americas	17.37

Shot

			metres
1977	U Beyer	E Germany	21.74
1979	U Beyer	E Germany	20.45
1981	U Beyer	E Germany	21.40

Discus			metres
1977	W Schmidt	E Germany	67.14
1979	W Schmidt	E Germany	66.02
1981	A Lemme	E Germany	66.38

Hammer			metres
1977	K-H Reihm	W Germany	75.64
1979	S Litvinov	USSR	78.70
1981	Y Syedikh	USSR	77.42

Javelin			metres
1977	M Wessing	W Germany	87.46
1979	W Hanisch	E Germany	86.48
1981	D Kula	USSR	89.74

WOMEN

100 metres			sec
1977	M Gohr	E Germany	11.16
1979	E Ashford	USA	11.06
1981	E Ashford	USA	11.02

200 metres			sec
1977	I Szewinska	Europe	22.72
1979	E Ashford	USA	21.83
1981	E Ashford	USA	22.18

400 metres			sec
1977	I Szewinska	Europe	49.52
1979	M Koch	E Germany	48.97
1981	J Kratochvilova	Europe	48.61

800 metres			min	sec
1977	T Petrova	Europe	1	59.2
1979	N Shtereva	Europe	2	00.6
1981	L Veselkova	USSR	1	57.48

1500 metres			min	sec
1977	T Kazankina	USSR	4	12.7
1979	C Watenberg	E Germany	4	06.9
1981	T Sorokina	USSR	4	03.33

3000 metres			min	sec
1977	G Waitz	Europe	8	43.5
1979	S Ulmasova	USSR	8	36.4
1981	A Zauber	E Germany	8	54.89

100 metres hurdles

			sec
1977	G Rabsztyn	Europe	12.70
1979	G Rabsztyn	Europe	12.67
1981	T Anisimova	USSR	12.85

400 metres hurdles

			sec
1979	B Klepp	E Germany	55.83
1981	E Neumann	E Germany	54.82

4×100 metres relay

		sec
1977	Europe	42.51
1979	Europe	42.19
1981	E Germany	42.22

4×400 metres relay

		min	sec
1977	E Germany	3	24.0
1979	E Germany	3	20.4
1981	E Germany	3	20.62

High jump

			metres
1977	R Ackermann	E Germany	1.98
1979	D Brill	Americas	1.96
1981	U Meyfarth	Europe	1.96

Long jump

			metres
1977	L Jacenko	Oceania	6.54
1979	A Stukane	USSR	6.64
1981	S Ulbricht	E Germany	6.80

Shot

			metres
1977	I Slupianek	E Germany	20.93
1979	I Slupianek	E Germany	20.98
1981	I Slupianek	E Germany	20.60

Discus

			metres
1977	F Melnik	USSR	68.10
1979	E Jahl	E Germany	65.18
1981	E Jahl	E Germany	66.70

Javelin

			metres
1977	R Fuchs	E Germany	62.36
1979	R Fuchs	E Germany	66.10
1981	A Todorova	Europe	70.08

EUROPA CUP

OVERALL TEAM RESULTS

MEN

1965 Stuttgart		points
1	USSR	86
2	W Germany	85
3	Poland	69
4	E Germany	69
5	France	60
6	Great Britain	48

1967 Kiev		
1	USSR	81
2	W Germany	80
3	E Germany	80
4	Poland	68
5	France	57
6	Hungary	53

(GB eliminated in semi finals)

1970 Stockholm		
1	E Germany	102
2	USSR	92½
3	W Germany	91
4	Poland	82
5	France	77½
6	Sweden	68
7	Italy	47

(GB eliminated in semi finals)

1973 Edinburgh		
1	USSR	82½
2	E Germany	78½
3	W Germany	76
4	Great Britain	71½
5	Finland	64½
6	France	45

1975 Nice		
1	E Germany	112
2	USSR	109
3	Poland	101
4	Great Britain	83
5	W Germany	83
6	Finland	83
7	France	80
8	Italy	68

WOMEN

Kassel		points
1	USSR	56
2	E Germany	42
3	Poland	38
4	W Germany	37
5	Hungary	32
6	Netherlands	26

1	USSR	51
2	E Germany	43
3	W Germany	36
4	Poland	35
5	Great Britain	34
6	Hungary	32

Budapest		
1	E Germany	70
2	W Germany	63
3	USSR	43
4	Poland	33
5	Great Britain	32
6	Hungary	32

1	E Germany	72
2	USSR	52
3	Bulgaria	50
4	W Germany	36
5	Great Britain	36
6	Rumania	27

1	E Germany	97
2	USSR	77
3	W Germany	65
4	Poland	58
5	Rumania	47
6	Bulgaria	47
7	Great Britain	40
8	France	36

	1977 Helsinki	**points**			**points**
1	E Germany	125	1	E Germany	106
2	W Germany	112	2	USSR	94
3	USSR	100	3	Great Britain	68
4	Great Britain	95	4	W Germany	68
5	Poland	93	5	Poland	58
6	France	70	6	Rumania	55
7	Finland	66	7	Bulgaria	53
8	Italy	54	8	Finland	36

	1979 Turin				
1	E Germany	125	1	E Germany	102
2	USSR	114	2	USSR	100
3	W Germany	110	3	Bulgaria	76
4	Poland	90	4	Great Britain	62
5	Great Britain	82	5	Rumania	58
6	Italy	79	6	W Germany	58
7	France	70½	7	Poland	55
8	Yugoslavia	49½	8	Italy	29

	1981 Zagreb				
1	E Germany	128	1	E Germany	108½
2	USSR	124½	2	USSR	97
3	Great Britain	106½	3	W Germany	74
4	W Germany	97	4	Great Britain	74
5	Italy	75	5	Bulgaria	72
6	Poland	74	6	Poland	53½
7	France	71	7	Hungary	41
8	Yugoslavia	41	8	Yugoslavia	20

	1983 Crystal Palace				
1	E Germany	117	1	E Germany	107
2	USSR	106	2	USSR	85
3	W Germany	102	3	Czechoslovakia	77
4	Great Britain	93½	4	Great Britain	77
5	Poland	91½	5	Bulgaria	58
6	Italy	80½	6	W Germany	57
7	France	69	7	Poland	42
8	Hungary	59½	8	Hungary	37

MEN

100 metres

			sec
1965	M Dudziak	Poland	10.3
1967	V Sapeya	USSR	10.3
1970	Z Nowosz	Poland	10.4
1973	S Schenke	E Germany	10.26
1975	V Borzov	USSR	10.40
1977	E Ray	E Germany	10.12
1979	P Mennea	Italy	10.15

1981	A Wells	GB		10.17
1983	F Emmelmann	E Germany		10.58

200 metres

				sec
1965	J Schwarz	W Germany		21.1
1967	J-C Nallet	France		20.9
1970	S Schenke	E Germany		20.7
1973	C Monk	GB		21.0
1975	P Mennea	Italy		20.42
1977	E Ray	E Germany		20.86
1979	A Wells	GB		20.29
1981	F Emmelmann	E Germany		20.33
1983	A Wells	GB		20.72

400 metres

				sec
1965	A Badenski	Poland		45.9
1967	J-C Nallet	France		46.3
1970	J Werner	Poland		45.9
1973	K Honz	W Germany		45.20
1975	D Jenkins	GB		45.52
1977	B Hermann	W Germany		45.92
1979	H Schmid	W Germany		45.31
1981	H Weber	W Germany		45.32
1983	H Weber	W Germany		45.39

800 metres

			min	sec
1965	F-J Kemper	W Germany	1	50.3
1967	M Matuschewski	E Germany	1	46.9
1970	Y Arzhanov	USSR	1	47.8
1973	A Carter	GB	1	46.8
1975	S Ovett	GB	1	46.6
1977	W Wulbeck	W Germany	1	47.2
1979	S Coe	GB	1	47.3
1981	S Coe	GB	1	47.03
1983	W Wulbeck	W Germany	1	45.74

1500 metres

			min	sec
1965	B Tummler	W Germany	3	47.4
1967	M Matuschewski	E Germany	3	40.2
1970	F Arese	Italy	3	42.3
1973	F Clements	GB	3	40.8
1975	T Wessinghage	W Germany	3	39.1
1977	S Ovett	GB	3	44.9
1979	J Straub	E Germany	3	36.3
1981	O Beyer	E Germany	3	43.52
1983	S Cram	GB	3	42.27

5000 metres

			min	sec
1965	H Norpoth	W Germany	14	18.0

1967	H Norpoth	W Germany	15	26.8
1970	H Norpoth	W Germany	14	25.4
1973	B Foster	GB	13	54.8
1975	B Foster	GB	13	36.2
1977	N Rose	GB	13	27.8
1979	H-J Kunze	E Germany	14	12.9
1981	D Moorcroft	GB	13	43.18
1983	T Wessinghage	W Germany	13	48.72

10,000 metres

			min	sec
1965	N Dutov	USSR	28	42.2
1967	J Haase	E Germany	28	54.2
1970	J Haase	E Germany	28	26.8
1973	N Sviridov	USSR	28	44.2
1975	K-H Leiteritz	E Germany	28	37.2
1977	J Peter	E Germany	27	55.5
1979	B Foster	GB	28	22.9
1981	W Schildhauer	E Germany	28	45.89
1983	W Schildhauer	E Germany	28	02.11

3000 metres steeplechase

			min	sec
1965	V Kudinskiy	USSR	8	41.0
1967	A Kuryan	USSR	8	38.8
1970	V Dudin	USSR	8	31.6
1973	T Kantanen	Finland	8	28.6
1975	M Karst	W Germany	8	16.4
1977	M Karst	W Germany	8	27.9
1979	M Scartezzini	Italy	8	22.8
1981	M Scartezzini	Italy	8	13.32
1983	B Maminski	Poland	8	24.80

110 metres hurdles

			sec
1965	A Milhailov	USSR	13.9
1967	V Balikhin	USSR	14.0
1970	G Drut	France	13.7
1973	G Drut	France	13.70
1975	G Drut	France	13.57
1977	T Munkelt	E Germany	13.37
1979	T Munkelt	E Germany	13.47
1981	M Holtom	GB	13.79
1983	T Munkelt	E Germany	13.72

400 metres hurdles

			sec
1965	R Poirier	France	50.8
1967	G Hennige	W Germany	50.2
1970	J-C Nallet	France	50.1
1973	A Pascoe	GB	50.07
1975	A Pascoe	GB	49.0
1977	V Beck	E Germany	48.90

1979	H Schmid	W Germany		47.85
1981	V Beck	E Germany		48.94
1983	H Schmid	W Germany		48.56

4 × 100 metres relay

				sec
1965	USSR			39.4
1967	France			39.2
1970	E Germany			39.4
1973	E Germany			39.45
1975	E Germany			38.98
1977	E Germany			38.84
1979	Poland			38.47
1981	Poland			38.66
1983	Italy			38.86

4 × 400 metres relay

			min	sec
1965	W Germany		3	08.3
1967	Poland		3	04.4
1970	Poland		3	05.1
1973	W Germany		3	04.3
1975	Great Britain		3	02.9
1977	W Germany		3	02.7
1979	W Germany		3	02.0
1981	Italy		3	01.42
1983	Great Britain		3	02.28

High jump

			metres
1965	V Brumel	USSR	2.15
1967	V Garilov	USSR	2.09
1970	K Lundmark	Sweden	2.15
1973	V Gavrilov	USSR	2.15
1975	A Grigoryev	USSR	2.24
1977	R Beilschmidt	E Germany	2.31
1979	D Mogenburg	W Germany	2.32
1981	V Sereda	USSR	2.30
1983	F Verzy	France	2.32

Pole vault

			metres
1965	W Nordwig	E Germany	5.0
1967	W Nordwig	E Germany	5.10
1970	W Nordwig	E Germany	5.35
1973	A Kalliomaki & Y Assakov	Finland USSR	5.30
1975	W Kozakiewicz	Poland	5.45
1977	W Kozakiewicz	Poland	5.60
1979	K Volkov	USSR	5.60
1981	J-M Bellot & K Volkov	France USSR	5.40
1983	P Abada	France	5.55

Long jump			metres
1965	I Ter-Ovanesyan	USSR	7.87
1967	I Ter-Ovanesyan	USSR	8.14
1970	J Pani	France	8.09
1973	V Podluzhny	USSR	8.20
1975	G Cybulski	Poland	8.15
1977	J Rousseau	France	8.05
1979	L Dombrowski	E Germany	8.31
1981	U Lange	E Germany	7.98
1983	L Szalma	Hungary	8.10

Triple jump			metres
1965	H-J Ruckborn	E Germany	16.51
1967	V Sanyeyev	USSR	16.67
1970	J Drehmel	E Germany	17.13
1973	V Sanyeyev	USSR	16.90
1975	V Sanyeyev	USSR	16.97
1977	A Piskulin	USSR	17.09
1979	B Lamitie	France	16.94
1981	J Uudmae	USSR	16.97
1983	P Bouschen	W Germany	17.12

Shot			metres
1965	N Karasyov	USSR	19.19
1967	V Varju	Hungary	19.25
1970	H Briesenick	E Germany	20.55
1973	H Briesenick	E Germany	20.95
1975	G Capes	GB	20.75
1977	U Beyer	E Germany	21.65
1979	U Beyer	E Germany	21.13
1981	U Beyer	E Germany	21.41
1983	E Sarul	Poland	20.54

Discus			metres
1965	Z Begier	Poland	58.92
1967	E Piatkowski	Poland	59.10
1970	R Bruch	Sweden	64.88
1973	P Kahma	Finland	63.10
1975	W Schmidt	E Germany	63.16
1977	W Schmidt	E Germany	66.86 *
1979	W Schmidt	E Germany	66.76
1981	A Lemme	E Germany	64.06
1983	J Schult	E Germany	64.96

* M Tuokko (Finland) 67.06 disqualified

Hammer			metres
1965	R Klim	USSR	67.70
1967	R Klim	USSR	70.58

1970	A Bondarchuk	USSR	70.46
1973	A Bondarchuk	USSR	74.08
1975	K-H Riehm	W Germany	77.50
1977	K-H Riehm	W Germany	75.90
1979	K-H Riehm	W Germany	78.66
1981	Y Sedykh	USSR	77.68
1983	S Litvinov	USSR	81.52

Javelin			**metres**
1965	J Lusis	USSR	82.56
1967	J Lusis	USSR	85.38
1970	W Nikiciuk	Poland	82.46
1973	K Wolfermann	W Germany	90.68
1975	N Grebnyev	USSR	84.30
1977	N Grebnyev	USSR	87.18
1979	W Hanisch	E Germany	88.68
1981	D Michel	E Germany	90.86
1983	D Michel	E Germany	85.72

WOMEN

100 metres			**sec**
1965	E Klobukowski	Poland	11.3
1967	I Szewinska	Poland	11.2
1970	I Mickler	W Germany	11.3
1973	R Stecher	E Germany	11.25
1975	R Stecher	E Germany	11.29
1977	M Gohr	E Germany	11.07
1979	M Gohr	E Germany	11.03
1981	M Gohr	E Germany	11.17
1983	M Gohr	E Germany	11.28

200 metres			**sec**
1965	E Klobukowski	Poland	23.0
1967	I Szewinska	Poland	23.0
1970	R Stecher	E Germany	23.1
1973	R Stecher	E Germany	22.81
1975	R Stecher	E Germany	22.63
1977	I Szewinska	Poland	22.71
1979	L Kondratyeva	USSR	22.40
1981	B Wockel	E Germany	22.19
1983	J Kratochvilova	Czech	22.40

400 metres			**sec**
1965	M Itkina	USSR	54.0
1967	L Board	GB	53.7
1970	H Fischer	E Germany	53.2
1973	M Zehrt	E Germany	51.75

1975	I Szewinska	Poland		50.50
1977	M Koch	E Germany		49.53
1979	M Koch	E Germany		48.60
1981	M Koch	E Germany		49.43
1983	T Kocembova	Czech		49.33

800 metres

			min	sec
1965	H Suppe	E Germany	2	04.3
1967	L Erik	USSR	2	06.8
1970	H Falck	W Germany	2	04.9
1973	G Hoffmeister	E Germany	1	58.9
1975	M Suman	Rumania	2	00.6
1977	C Liebetrau	E Germany	2	00.2
1979	N Shtereva	Bulgaria	1	56.3
1981	M Steuk	E Germany	1	57.16
1983	J Kratochvilova	Czech	1	58.79

1500 metres

			min	sec
1970	E Tittel	W Germany	4	16.3
1973	T Petrova	Bulgaria	4	09.0
1975	W Strotzer	E Germany	4	08.0
1977	T Kazankina	USSR	4	04.4
1979	T Petrova	Bulgaria	4	03.2
1981	T Sorokina	USSR	4	01.37
1983	N Ralldugina	USSR	4	07.61

3000 metres

			min	sec
1981	A Zauber	E Germany	8	49.61
1983	T Kazankina	USSR	8	49.27

80 metres hurdles

			sec
1965	I Press	USSR	10.4
1967	K Balzer	E Germany	10.8

100 metres hurdles

			sec
1970	K Balzer	E Germany	13.1
1973	A Ehrhardt	E Germany	12.95
1975	A Ehrhardt	E Germany	12.83
1977	J Klier	E Germany	12.83
1979	T Anisimova	USSR	12.77
1981	T Anisimova	USSR	12.91
1983	B Jahn	E Germany	12.89

400 metres hurdles

			sec
1981	E Neumann	E Germany	54.90
1983	E Fiedler	E Germany	54.20

4×100 metres relay		sec
1965	Poland	44.9
1967	USSR	45.0
1970	W Germany	43.9
1973	E Germany	42.95
1975	E Germany	42.81
1977	E Germany	42.62
1979	E Germany	42.09
1981	E Germany	42.53
1983	E Germany	42.63

4×400 metres relay		min	sec
1970	E Germany	3	37.0
1973	E Germany	3	28.7
1975	E Germany	3	24.0
1977	E Germany	3	23.7
1979	E Germany	3	19.7
1981	E Germany	3	19.83
1983	Czechoslovakia	3	20.79

High jump			metres
1965	T Chenchik	USSR	1.70
1967	A Okerokova	USSR	1.79
1970	R Schmidt	E Germany	1.84
1973	Y Blagoeva	Bulgaria	1.84
1975	R Ackermann	E Germany	1.94
1977	R Ackermann	E Germany	1.97
1979	R Ackermann	E Germany	1.99
1981	U Meyfarth	W Germany	1.94
1983	U Meyfarth	W Germany	2.03

Long jump			metres
1965	T Shchelkanova	USSR	6.68
1967	I Mickler	W Germany	6.63
1970	H Rosendahl	W Germany	6.80
1973	A Voigt	E Germany	6.63
1975	L Alfeyeva	USSR	6.76
1977	B Wujak	E Germany	6.76
1979	B Wujak	E Germany	6.89
1981	S Ulbricht	E Germany	6.86
1983	H Daute	E Germany	6.99

Shot			metres
1965	T Press	USSR	18.59
1967	N Chizhova	USSR	18.24
1970	N Chizhova	USSR	19.42
1973	N Chizhova	USSR	20.77
1975	M Adam	E Germany	21.32

1977	E Wilms	W Germany	20.01 *
1979	I Slupianek	E Germany	20.93
1981	I Slupianek	E Germany	21.12
1983	H Fibingerova	Czech	20.76

* Slupianek 21.20 disqualified after doping test

Discus			metres
1965	J Kleiber	Hungary	56.74
1967	K Illgen	E Germany	58.26
1970	K Illgen	E Germany	61.60
1973	F Melnik	USSR	69.48
1975	F Melnik	USSR	66.54
1977	F Melnik	USSR	68.08
1979	E Jahl	E Germany	68.92
1981	M Petkova-Vergova	Bulgaria	69.08
1983	M Opitz	E Germany	69.0

Javelin			metres
1965	Y Gorchakova	USSR	58.48
1967	D Jaworska	Poland	56.88
1970	R Fuchs	E Germany	60.60
1973	R Fuchs	E Germany	66.10
1975	R Fuchs	E Germany	64.80
1977	R Fuchs	E Germany	68.92
1979	E Raduly	Rumania	66.28
1981	A Todorova	Bulgaria	71.88
1983	F Whitbread	GB	69.04

Marlies Gohr (East Germany) has won the 100 metres in the last four Europa Cups.

119

THE RULES OF ATHLETICS

TRACK EVENTS

THE SPRINTS

Whether it be in the 100 metres, where power and short-term energy are all-important, or the 400 metres, where sustained energy is needed to avoid the burn-out over the final 200 metres, the technique in sprints is very much in the hands of the coaches. The rules are basically very simple.

The Start

The first command is 'On your marks', the second is 'get set'. A gap of two seconds between 'set' and when the gun goes, is estimated as giving the best chance of a fast, fair start.

Many a fine race has been ruined by the delaying of the gun. If the runners in their blocks are given longer than two seconds, inevitably false starts occur. Each athlete is allowed just one, the second means instant dismissal.

Starting blocks are now linked by a sensory mechanism with the automatic timing system; they are sensitive to the slightest pressures. Any runner putting pressure on the blocks inside a tenth of a second after the gun, is penalized for a false start. In the case of major championships, only when all eight or nine have got it right will it be declared a legal start.

A runner who follows another competitor in a false start is not necessarily judged to have made a false start, if in the opinion of the starter he was triggered off by the original offender.

All competitors must have both feet in contact with the blocks and both hands in contact with the ground, behind the start-line.

The race

All sprints are run in lanes, with a staggered start in races that include bends. During the race runners must not 'creep' from their assigned lane, or run on a line. This offence often goes unnoticed by spectators, but there are judges round the track to pick up offenders.

The finish

The torso of the runner is the decider on the line, which is why athletes 'dip' as they approach the finish. A cotton tape is there to mark the finish and to help judges in their assessment, but it is only a guide, as the tape may billow in the wind.

MIDDLE-DISTANCE RACES

In races of 800 metres and over, starting blocks are not used. The 800 metres has a staggered start and is run in lanes as far as the end of the first bend. At this point, there is often a great deal of jostling as the runners break for a place on the inside. For individual races over 800 metres, the starting line is curved, so that all runners start the same distance from the finish.

The middle-distance events are often the subject of rough tactics, especially from around the bell, which is sounded to signal the last lap. Competition has always been fierce, but it is only in recent years that pushing and shoving have become accepted as part and parcel of the events. But such tactics have brought very few disqualifications. Provided that a runner is not actually fighting or overstepping the inside of the track, then first to the line is the winner.

THE MARATHON

Possibly the most heartbreaking instance of the rules being broken in this event came during the 1908 Olympic Games in London, when Dorando Pietri of Italy, leading the field, fell during the final hundred yards to the finish in White City Stadium. He was lifted to his feet by an official, carried away by the hysteria of the crowd. Pietri was disqualified.

World records cannot be officially instituted because of the variable shapes and gradients of courses. How, for example, could one compare the streets of New York to the climbs of the Isle of Wight?

The marathon must be run on hard roads. Only one turning point is allowed if it is not a straight course or a circuit. It must always finish in a stadium, though this rule has latterly been relaxed. The London Marathon, for example, does not finish in a stadium, and this event is recognized by official bodies such as the AAA and the BAAB, who use it as their official championships and major games trial.

One less well-known rule, possibly through determination rather than ignorance, is that any competitor deemed to be unfit or unwell by the medical staff, either before or during the race, must immediately withdraw.

Organizers must ensure that there are adequate refreshments provided at 5-km intervals. In addition, sponging points and water-only points are usually provided. Competitors taking refreshments at unofficial points are liable to be disqualified.

HURDLES

It is often said that it is hard enough to run a sprint without having hurdles in the way. The stride pattern becomes the vital element, for many a good sprinter has failed at the hurdles because of an inability to reach the obstacle on the correct foot, and so ensure a perfect landing on the other side.

Hurdle races are run in lanes, with 10 hurdles. The height of the hurdles is 1.067m (3ft 6in) for men's 110 metres, 0.914m (3ft) for men's 400 metres, 0.84m (2ft 9in) for the women's 100 metres, and 0.762m (2ft 6in) for the women's 400 metres. The rules for sprints on starts and finishes apply equally to hurdle races.

Although the rules stress that all hurdles must be cleared and that the deliberate knocking-down of an obstacle will lead to disqualification, many major races have been won by competitors who have left behind them a trail of devastation.

Athletes must keep to their own lanes and go over the hurdles, rather than around them. The one-lap event has a tendency to bring more disqualitications because of the rear leg coming outside the barrier on the curve of the bend.

STEEPLECHASE

Once the 'joke' event of athletics, used mainly to entertain rather than thrill the crowds, the steeplechase was often included in the programme with little regard for the safety of runners. On occasions, free-for-alls broke out during the running, the winner often arriving battered and bruised and frequently bleeding. But when it was included in the 1920 Olympics over the distance of 3,000 metres, it established its place in the athletics schedule.

The rules are basically those imposed on the running and hurdling events. There are 28 hurdles and seven water jumps in the standard 3,000 metres steeplechase. The barriers are 0.914m (3ft) high. From the start to the beginning of the first lap there are no hurdles, so that runners have time to sort themselves out before they attempt obstacles. The water jump, which is set off the track, is the fourth jump of each lap.

Every competitor must go over or through the water at the water jump, and over every hurdle by hurdling, jumping, or vaulting them. A foot may be placed on a hurdle.

RELAYS

The aim of relays is to get the baton from the start to the finish in the quickest possible time within the rules. The usual rules relating to sprinting apply — starting blocks, starter's commands, the necessity of athletes staying in their lanes, and the judging and timing of the finish.

Each of the four team members runs one stage of the race. A baton, a smooth hollow tube that weighs not less than 50g (1¾oz), is carried in the hand and transferred from athlete to athlete. It must be passed and not thrown. The second, third, and final runners in the relay team get a moving start and the baton is exchanged in either an upsweep or a downsweep action. If the baton is dropped, it has to be picked up where it fell by the athlete who dropped it, without impeding another runner. For each change, there is a 20m (22yd) take-over zone.

Relay races of 4×100 metres are run entirely in lanes, while 4×400 metre races are run in lanes as far as the exit from the first bend of the second lap. Competitors must return to their lanes for the baton take-over, unless they can use the inside lane without causing obstruction. After handing over the baton, athletes should stay in their lanes or zones until the course is clear. Teams may be disqualified for causing obstruction or giving assistance at take-overs.

JUMPING EVENTS

HIGH JUMP

The high jump was revolutionized in the mid-sixties when Dick Fosbury introduced his famous 'flop'. Most competitors now use either the Fosbury flop or the straddle.

Aids have been developed to improve height clearance, such as the famous built-up shoes produced by the Russians in the fifties. They were subsequently outlawed by the IAAF, who restricted thickness of soles to 13mm (½ in).

Starting heights for each round are announced by the judges before the event begins. Competitors may start jumping when they wish, and choose whether or not to attempt any subsequent height. Elimination occurs after three failures in a row, regardless of the height.

The basic rules are simple enough. A competitor fails if the bar is dislodged or if he or she touches the ground beyond the upright without first clearing the bar, or takes off from both feet.

If there is a tie, several competitors finishing on the same height, the winner is determined by the 'countback system'. The athlete with the fewest attempts at the final height cleared is the winner. If a winner cannot be gained from that, the competitor with the fewest total failures is declared the winner. These countback rules decide all tied places. But if the countback does not decide first place, the tied competitors have one more jump at the lower height failed; if no decision is reached, the bar can then be raised or lowered. They will attempt one more jump at each height until it is decided.

The high jump and the pole vault differ from other field events for they continue until a decision is reached.

POLE VAULT

It is said that all pole vaulters should be a little mad, for that is a definite advantage if you plan to hurl yourself over heights exceeding 19 feet and come crashing down again.

It is often a frustrating event, in which a vaulter, trying to conserve energy, misses out on earlier rounds, only to fail at his chosen height. Starting heights are announced by the judges before the event begins. Competitors may start vaulting when they choose, and choose whether or not to try any subsequent height. Elimination occurs after three consecutive failures, regardless of the height at which they occur.

A failure is counted if an athlete touches the ground beyond the vertical plane of the stopboard, including the landing area, with his pole or body; knocks the bar off the supports with his pole or body; leaves the ground to vault but fails to clear the bar; after leaving the ground places his lower hand above the upper one, or moves his upper hand up the pole; or if anyone else touches the pole as it falls towards the crossbar or uprights. If a competitor's pole breaks, it does not count as a failure.

LONG JUMP

It is no surprise that many sprinters, such as Carl Lewis, make superb long jumpers, for the basic ingredient is maximum controlled speed along the runway before take-off. Just like an aircraft taking off, the essential speed must be reached just before the take-off point. Failure to get it right at that point means an abortive attempt.

The aim is to capture as much of the six-inch board as possible, without overstepping it. It may look simple to the spectator, but it is far from that, for speed must not be sacrificed for lift, and wind conditions play an important part in success or failure.

Each competitor has six trials. In large competitions, each competitor will have three trials, then the best eight will have a further three. The competitor with the longest jump over his or her six trials is the winner.

The jump is measured from the farthest backward point of landing, back to the take-off line and at right-angles with that line. An athlete's jump is counted a failure if he or she oversteps the line. The area beyond the board is marked with a material such as plasticine that imprints the step, so avoiding any doubts either by judges or athletes.

No form of somersaulting is allowed. No weights may be carried. If an athlete walks back through the pit, then his or her jump is immediately called a foul.

Wind speeds of 2 metres per second and over invalidate any record. In the event of a tie, the athlete with the next best jump is declared the winner.

TRIPLE JUMP

The triple jump, also referred to as the hop, step, and jump, has the same basic rules as the long jump. In addition, the rules specify that the hop must be made from the take-off foot, back onto the same foot, and that the step must be made from the opposite foot. A foul is declared for overstepping the board or if the 'sleeping' leg touches the ground at any time.

THROWING EVENTS

The rules for all four throwing events, the shot, the discus, the hammer, and the javelin — are very similar and can be outlined together.

The shot and hammer are thrown from a 2.135m (7ft) circle, with the shot circle fronted by a stop-board. The discus is thrown from a 2.50m (8ft 2½ in) diameter circle. Any infringement of the rim (or in the case of the shot, the stop-board) will result in a foul throw.

No competitor may leave the circle until the implement has landed. They must retreat from the rear half of the circle. Measurements are always made from the farthest back mark made by the implement, back through the centre of the circle. The distance is read over the front rim.

In javelin, similar rules apply. The areas at the side of the runway are also forbidden to the thrower after his throw. Distances are measured to the scratch line.

Each competitor generally has six throws. If there are more than eight competitors, some are eliminated after the first three trials. A tie for first place is decided by the competitors' second-best trials.

THE SHOT

In making his puts, the competitor may rest his feet against, but not on top of, the stop-board. The shot must be put from the shoulder with one hand only. At the time of beginning a trial, the shot must touch or be in close proximity to the chin and the hand may not be dropped below this level during the action. The shot may not be taken behind the line of the shoulders. The men's shot weighs 7.26kg (16lb), the women's 4kg (8.82lb).

For a shot to be valid, it must fall so that the point from which measurement is taken lies within an area which makes a sector of 45 degrees from the centre of the throwing circle.

THE DISCUS

All discus throws are made from an enclosure or cage. For a throw to be valid, it must land so that the point of measurement falls within a sector of 45 degrees from the centre of the throwing circle. The men's discus weighs 2kg (4.4lb), the women's 1kg (2.2lb). The diameter of the men's discus is 22cm (8.66in), the women's 18cm (7.09in).

THE HAMMER

Hammer throws are made from a cage, into an area of 45 degrees from the centre of the throwing circle. The competitor in his starting position, prior to his preliminary swings, is allowed to put the head of the hammer inside or outside the circle, on the ground. The hammer weighs 7.26kg (16lb) and is attached to the grip by steel wire about 120cm (47in) long.

THE JAVELIN

All throws, to be valid, must fall within an area set out on the ground and extending in an arc of 29 degrees from the centre point (8 metres behind the scratch line). No throw will be valid unless the tip of the metal head strikes the ground first, but it does not have to stick in the ground.

The javelin must be held with one hand only, at the grip, so the little finger is nearest to the point. The javelin must be thrown over the shoulder or upper part of the throwing arm, and must not be slung or hurled. The athlete must not turn his or her back to the arc before preparing to throw and letting the javelin go.

The men's javelin measures 2.6—2.7m (8ft 6in—8ft 10in), the women's 2.2—2.3m (7ft 2½in—7ft 6½in).

COMBINED COMPETITIONS

THE DECATHLON

The decathlon is a men's competition of ten events. Competitors score points for their performance in each event. The points are not awarded for placings, but for achieving set times, heights, and distances against a certain standard.

Daley Thompson (GB), who has dominated decathlon championships since 1980.

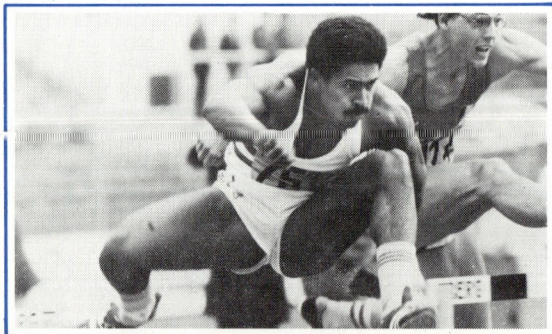

The rules for each event apply, with the exceptions that competitors are allowed only three trials in each field event, and three false starts in a track event will mean elimination. A competitor is considered to have withdrawn from the competition if he fails to participate in any event. The events are held in a set order over two days.

First day: 100m, long jump, shot, high jump, 400m
Second day: 110m hurdles, discus, pole vault, javelin, 1500m

The leaders of the event are segregated into pools or sections until the last event, when they are drawn together. Ties in the decathlon are rare, but if it does happen, the winner is the man who in the greater number of events has scored more points than the other competitor(s) tying.

DECATHLON POINTS TABLE
First Day

Points	100 m	long jump	shot put	high jump	400 m
500	12.5 sec	5.54 m 18ft 2in	10.55 m 34ft 7¼in	1.60 m 5ft 3in	57.9 sec
600	12.0 sec	5.98 m 19ft 7½in	12.01 m 39ft 4¾in	1.71 m 5ft 7½in	55.1 sec
700	11.5 sec	6.43 m 21ft 1in	13.55 m 44ft 5½in	1.82 m 5ft 11½in	52.5 sec
800	11.1 sec	6.90 m 22ft 7½in	15.19 m 49ft 10in	1.93 m 6ft 4in	50.2 sec
900	10.7 sec	7.39 m 24ft 3in	16.92 m 55ft 6in	2.05 m 6ft 8¾in	48.0 sec
1000	10.3 sec	7.90 m 25ft 11in	18.75 m 61ft 6¼in	2.17 7ft 1½in	46.0 sec

Second Day

Points	110 m hurdles	discus	pole vault	javelin	1500 m
500	19.2 sec	31.14 m 102ft 2in	2.90 m 9ft 6¼in	40.59 m 133ft 2in	4min 44.0sec
600	17.8 sec	35.77 m 117ft 4in	3.24 m 10ft 7½in	47.56 m 156ft 1in	4min 28.4sec
700	16.6 sec	40.72 m 133ft 7in	3.60 m 11ft 9¾in	55.09 m 180ft 9in	4min 14.5sec
800	15.5 sec	45.99 m 150ft 10in	3.97 m 13ft 0¼in	63.17 m 207ft 3in	4min 02.0sec
900	14.6 sec	51.58 m 169ft 2in	4.36 m 14ft 3½in	71.81 m 235ft 7in	3min 50.6sec
1000	13.7 sec	57.50 m 188ft 7in	4.78 m 15ft 8in	81.00 m 265ft 9in	3min 40.2sec

THE HEPTATHLON

The women's combined competition was augmented in 1981 for major championships from the five-event pentathlon to the seven-event heptathlon, held over two days.

First day: 100m hurdles, high jump, shot, 200m
Second day: long jump, javelin, 800m

HEPTATHLON POINTS TABLE

First Day

Points	100m hurdles	high jump	shot put	200m
600	16.48 sec	1.39m	10.16m	28.17 sec
700	15.45 sec	1.48m	11.69m	26.79 sec
800	14.54 sec	1.57m	13.34m	25.54 sec
900	13.73 sec	1.67m	15.09m	24.40 sec
1000	13.01 sec	1.77m	16.95m	23.36 sec

Second Day

Points	long jump	javelin	800m
600	4.69m	30.06m	2min 36.9sec
700	5.10m	35.86m	2min 27.5sec
800	5.53m	42.18m	2min 19.2sec
900	5.97m	49m	2min 11.8sec
1000	6.44m	56.34m	2min 5.1sec

WALKING

Possibly, the most controversial event of all is the walking, where the naked eye is used to detect the 'cheats' — those who do not 'heel and toe' around the course. While the techniques are innumerable, the rules are simplified by stating 'unbroken contact' with the ground must be maintained at all times — that is, the advancing foot must be in contact with the ground before the rear foot leaves the ground. And during the period of each step in which a foot is on the ground, the leg must be straightened (i.e. not bent at the knee) at least for one moment, and. . . the supporting leg must be straight in the vertically upright position. Infringements of this action, 'lifting' or 'creeping', may lead to disqualification.

A walker can be cautioned during the race for a doubtful action. If it continues, two judges, one of whom is the chief judge, or alternatively three judges, are required for a disqualification. There is no such luxury as a second warning. The disqualified competitor must leave the track immediately.

Approved refreshments may be taken at official refreshment stations in walking races over 20 kilometres.